The Illegal Images Workbook

Understanding and Changing Harmful Online Sexual Behavior

David L. Delmonico, Ph.D., LPC & Elizabeth J. Griffin, MA, LMFT

ISBN: 979-8-218-59214-1

An Introduction

Welcome to Our Therapeutic Workbook

We created this workbook because we recognize that the use of child sexual abuse media (CSAM) is a serious issue. We understand that your decision to purchase this workbook was not an easy one. After all, choosing to engage in this process requires courage and self-reflection. However, the fact that you have taken this step is a strong indication of your willingness and motivation to address a difficult issue. Whether you are currently involved in the legal system or seeking to avoid legal consequences, we believe this workbook will be a valuable resource for you.

You should know that you are not alone in facing these challenges—otherwise, why would we create this workbook? Many others struggle with similar issues, and acknowledging the problem is the first step toward change.

Our inspiration for writing this workbook comes from our experiences working with individuals like you—people who feel shame, fear, and distress about their behaviors and who face the personal and legal consequences of their actions. At the same time, we know that many of these individuals seek **Awareness, Health, Freedom, and Hope** (as represented by the signpost on the cover) to break free from harmful patterns.

This workbook is designed to provide you with information, exercises, and resources to help you navigate a new path—one that leads away from harmful content and toward a healthier and more fulfilling life. We aim to strike a balance between increasing your awareness and helping you develop new skills to change your behavior.

Our goal is to support you in becoming a person who can manage emotions effectively, build healthy connections with others, engage in appropriate and fulfilling sexual behaviors, use technology in responsible ways, and fully understand the impact of child sexual abuse media on victims and society. While these goals may seem ambitious, we firmly believe that change is possible—and that you have the capacity to achieve it.

Words Are Important: A Few Key Definitions

Before moving forward, we need to ensure we have a shared understanding of the term "illegal images." In the United States, illegal child sexual abuse media refers to any image of a child under the age of 18 that depicts their genitalia or portrays a child engaged in any form of sexual behavior. If you are reading this book in another country, different legal definitions may apply, but most nations have similar laws prohibiting such content.

This type of media is often referred to as "child pornography." However, we strongly encourage you to avoid using that term. Instead, we ask you to replace it with "child sexual abuse media." The reason for this shift in terminology is that "child sexual abuse media" serves as a constant reminder that the children depicted in such images are victims of abuse. Using acronyms such as CP or CSAM can unintentionally minimize the severity of the harm involved, and we want to reinforce that **viewing child sexual abuse media is not a victimless act.**

Although the phrase "child sexual abuse media" may feel cumbersome or grammatically awkward at times, we will consistently use it throughout this workbook. Our goal is not to shame you, but rather to help ensure that the impact on the children involved is never minimized.

It is also important to recognize that even if you are not viewing illegal child sexual abuse media, you may still struggle with sexualized images of children. Pornography can be broadly defined as any image viewed for sexual gratification or arousal. Some individuals may find themselves sexualizing fully clothed images of children, advertisements, TikTok videos, Facebook Reels, or other media featuring minors. If this is something you struggle with, this workbook will still be beneficial to you, and we commend your willingness to address this issue and commit to change.

Workbook Organization

This workbook is organized around six core areas: (1) emotion management, (2) i intimacy skills, (3) deviant sexuality (4) out of control sexual behavior, (5) technology use, and (6) victim awareness.

These areas were chosen because research indicates that they are common underlying factors in the use of child sexual abuse media. This does not mean that these are the only struggles individuals face, but they are among the most prevalent and, therefore, essential to address.

Before exploring these six key areas, the workbook begins with a chapter titled **"Building the Foundation."** This introductory chapter provides the fundamental knowledge needed to maximize the effectiveness of the material covered in the later sections.

We have designed this workbook to be interactive and engaging. We believe that the use of imagery and metaphors helps individuals retain information more effectively. Each exercise encourages you to **"Reflect & Respond"** and **"React"** to the concepts being presented, allowing for deeper understanding and personal growth.

Workbook Website

We have created a companion website to the workbook - *www.internetbehavior.com/illegalimages*. The website includes graphics, additional reading materials, and extra resources. We will continue to update the webpage periodically with new materials.

Feel free to check back often to see if we've added anything new!

We realize that some readers may be on probation and have restrictions for their technology use. Talk with your probation officer and/or your therapist to explore the possibilities of gaining access to the webpage. Your probation officer or therapist may be willing to sit with you as you review the information on the webpage or even allow you to print some of the resources from their office.

Helpful Advice

As you prepare to begin, we recommend keeping a notebook or journal handy to take notes as you work through the exercises. Having all your notes in one place will be helpful as you progress through the workbook. You may experience various thoughts, emotions, and even occasional moments of insight. You might also find it beneficial to share your notes with a therapist, probation officer, or accountability partner, or to revisit them as you continue working through the material.

You may also want to have a folder to store printed pages from the website or any pages you remove from your workbook. There are no rules against tearing out pages that are meaningful to you. A folder will help keep all your loose materials organized for later review.

While it is not required to work with a therapist while using this workbook, we **strongly** encourage it. The exercises in this workbook can only take you so far on their own, and a therapist can help you explore these concepts more deeply. In fact, engaging with this workbook while in therapy will likely enhance both experiences.

If you are unsure where to begin your search for a therapist, consider reaching out to **Stop It Now!** They provide resources and referrals for individuals seeking support.

1-888-773-8368 (888-PREVENT)
or
http://www.stopitnow.org

Keep in mind that you can request help anonymously. Staff at Stop It Now are familiar with addressing issues related to the use of child sexual abuse media and the sexual abuse of children.

Before We Start...

We want to thank a few people who were critical in the development of this workbook. Many individuals contributed by assisting with the workbook or allowing us to adapt exercises they developed.

First, we want to thank Dr. Patrick Carnes. Although our paths don't cross much anymore, we deeply appreciate your mentorship and encouragement. It helped us explore the world of problematic online sexual behavior. Plus, we never would have met without our common connection to you. Your wisdom is evident throughout the book, including in the Technology Craziness Index that appears in this workbook. Thank you for all you have done for us and for the field.

We also want to express our gratitude to our friend Jerry Fjerkenstad. Your steadfast support over the years has helped us see the world from a different perspective, and we love sharing your brilliant ideas with our readers.

Thank you to Debbie and Mark Laaser, who were often our biggest cheerleaders in getting things done. They also generously allowed us to borrow some of their best concepts that help clients understand their relationships with themselves, and others.

We also had the support of other colleagues, proofreaders, brainstormers, critical friends, graphic designers, and many others who helped bring this workbook together. So… if there's something you don't like in here, blame them. 😊

Finally, we want to thank our clients for trusting us with your stories and experiences over the years. Your honesty and willingness to allow us to witness your journey toward rebuilding integrity inspired this book. Thank you!

We would love to hear from you about your experiences with the workbook—positive, negative, or otherwise. Do you have an idea for our next workbook? Did any of the exercises stand out as particularly helpful? Was there one that didn't work for you? Let us know! You can email us at info@internetbehavior.com or send us a note via snail mail to 5115 Excelsior Boulevard, #450, Minneapolis, MN 55416.

Okay… enough rambling. Let's get started on your recovery journey.

Wishing you much success,

David & Elizabeth

Contents

Chapter 1: Building the Foundation

Let's get STARTED!!

This chapter will provide activities to assist you in building the foundation for understanding your use of child sexual abuse media. Understanding some of the basic concepts we believe are important is essential before moving on to the other chapter of the workbook. Throughout the workbook, we will refer back to and build on the concepts in this chapter.

A List of Chapter Exercises

1. Word Webs
2. No Trained Seals
3. The Attorney
4. The Change Process
5. The Seven Desires
6. The Inner Warrior
7. Hermes Web

Don't forget!

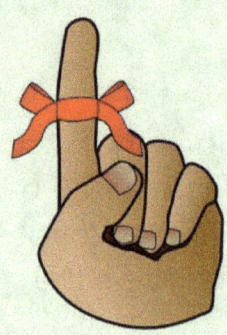

Those of you who have access to the Internet may want to visit our companion website for resources related to this and other chapters in the workbook. These resources may include additional articles, websites, and copies of activities/graphics from the chapters.

http://www.internetbehavior.com/illegalimages

Notes

_____

_____

_____

_____

_____

_____

_____

_____

_____

_____

Word Webs

A "word web" is a brainstorm of words that are related to a "base word," which is listed in the center of the web. These brainstormed words can be any type of word (adjectives, verbs, nouns, adverbs, etc.), so long as the word comes to mind when thinking about the base word. The example below shows a completed word web for the base word "Dog."

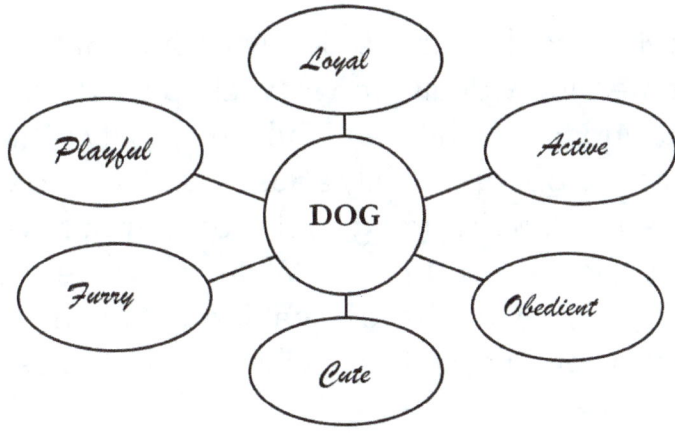

React

Now that you have seen an example, we want you to complete two different word webs. The first uses the base words "child pornography," and the second uses the base words "child sexual abuse media." Spend about 10 minutes on each word web. Feel free to draw additional circles on the page if needed.

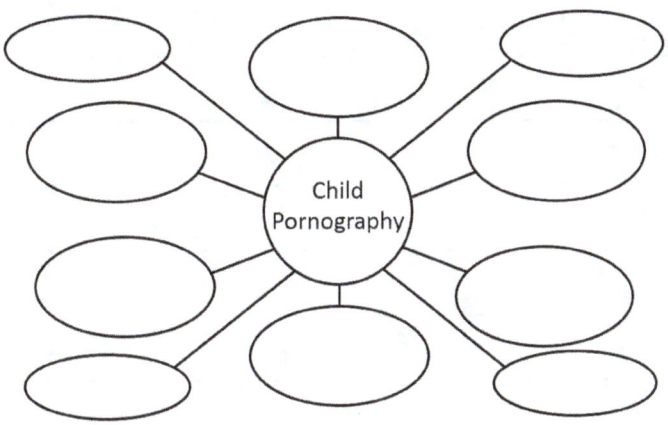

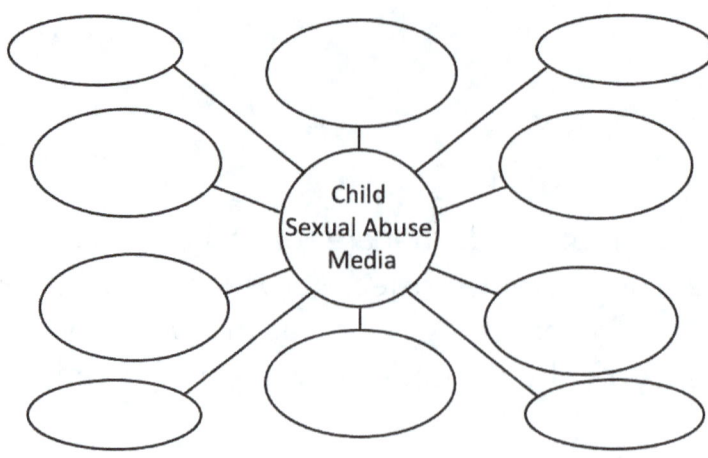

The purpose of this activity is to think more clearly about what child sexual abuse media truly represents. Sometimes, individuals who view child sexual abuse media will say, "I'm not as bad as those who touch children." Still, the reality is that children depicted in child sexual abuse media are being sexually abused. Even images/videos that appear to be "artistic" or are taken as "nudist" images/videos do not have the consent of the child to be posted online for sexual purposes. While computer-generated, hentai, and AI images/videos of children may not have a real-life victim, they often portray child sexual abuse or exploitation against children, which perpetuates the belief that the sexual abuse of children is ok.

Reflect & Respond

1. What similarities and differences do you notice between the two word webs you completed?

_____

_____

_____

_____

_____

_____

_____

2. What were some of the thoughts and emotions you felt while completing the word webs?

_____

_____

_____

3. Was one of the word webs more difficult to complete than the other? Explain your answer.

_____

_____

_____

4. Which base word more explicitly states what is happening in the illegal images/videos you have viewed?

_____

_____

_____

5. Is it difficult for you to understand how "sexualized" images/videos of children (even if they are not engaged in sexual acts) are equivalent to sexually exploiting a child?

_____

_____

_____

_____

_____

No Trained Seals!

While trained seals might be fun to watch at an aquarium, they are not fun when they represent how you interact with others.

The "No Trained Seal" image (below) represents the part in all of us that wants to say and do what will please others. This is not always a bad thing. But if you **only** say and do what you think will please others, it becomes difficult to identify **YOUR** genuine thoughts, feelings, needs, and wants in life.

It is easy to become a trained seal with others. There are many reasons why you might fall into the trap of being a trained seal.

- You don't want to disappoint those you care about and love.
- You don't want to cause problems for yourself and/or others.
- You fear conflict and find it easier to say/do what people want.
- You don't want to hurt others' feelings.
- You don't want to face the consequences of being honest.
- You want to be accepted/loved.
- You are afraid if you are yourself, others may be disgusted.

While being a trained seal can make you and everyone around you feel better in the short run, in the long run, you end up exhausted, unhappy, and more likely to "act out" in some way such as sexually acting out with your technology use.

It is important to note that it does not work well to be a trained seal in therapy! Unless your therapist knows what you truly think, feel, need, and want it is impossible to truly help you figure out why you are using child sexual abuse media. Also remember that staying in trained seal mode as you work through this workbook is going to limit the usefulness of the exercises.

Our hope is that you can discover **YOUR** genuine thoughts, feelings, needs, and wants in life as you move through the process of addressing your use of child sexual abuse media.

Reflect & Respond

1. Describe a time in your life when you acted like a trained seal. Is the trained seal pattern a common pattern for you?

_____

_____

_____

2. Are there certain people in your life that you fall into the trained seal pattern with more often? If so, why?

_____

_____

_____

_____

3. Above, we provided a list of reasons why people might choose to become a trained seal. Is there one reason on the list that stands out to you? Can you think of other reasons why you might become a trained seal? Are you more likely to be a trained seal when it comes to conversations about your sexuality and/or your use of child sexual abuse media?

_____

_____

_____

4. What are some of the benefits/problems in your life with being a trained seal?

_____

_____

_____

5. How does being a trained seal impact progress in treatment?

_____

_____

_____

_____

_____

_____

_____

_____

React

Develop a strategy to recognize when you are being a trained seal AND how you can make some attempts to stop being a trained seal with others.

Sometimes, it helps to break these habits by setting up an experiment with yourself. For example, you might say to yourself, "I am going to conduct an experiment today. I will consciously try not to be a trained seal with (name a person)." Or you might say, "Today at work, I'm going to reduce my trained seal responses by 50%."

Use these experiments to collect data about changing your trained seal behavior. How did others respond to you when you didn't act like a trained seal? How did you feel interacting differently with others? Could you do this more often? Maybe extend the experiment and try it again based on the new data you gather.

If you often fall into trained seal mode, we suggest buying a trained seal wind-up toy that you can keep on your desk, in your car, or perhaps on your kitchen counter. They are inexpensive and a great visual reminder to work on being more authentic!

Notes

_____

_____

_____

_____

_____

_____

The Attorney

Real Life Attorneys Are Helpful

They mediate.
They soften the blow.
They decide what should and should not be said.
They protect your best interest.
They present you in the best light possible.
They speak for you in legal language.
They advocate for and protect you in a difficult system.

However, Your "Inner Attorney" Is Not Always Helpful

They try to protect, defend you even when you are wrong.
They don't want you to tell the whole truth.
They are slow to trust that others can help.
They always assume others are out to get you.
They keep trying the case until the outcome is different.
They can make treatment take longer.

Your "Inner Attorney" Uses the Following Defense Strategies

Deny – I am not guilty.
Blame – It is not my fault.
Diversion Tactics – The system is messed up.
No one told me it was illegal.
Minimize – I didn't actually touch a child.
            Everyone looks at all kinds of porn online.

The "Inner Attorney"

Everyone has an "inner attorney." When we feel threatened, our "inner attorney" surfaces to protect, attack, defend, and/or delay. Everyone needs an "inner attorney." The goal is not to make the "inner attorney" go away, but rather to:

- Create awareness of your "inner attorney"
- Take responsibility for your "inner attorney" and their behaviors
- Effectively manage your "inner attorney"

Reflect & Respond

1. Describe your "inner attorney."

_____

_____

_____

_____

_____

_____

2. How did your "inner attorney" keep you from telling the entire truth about your viewing of child sexual abuse media? Is your "inner attorney" still working to keep you from telling the entire truth about viewing child sexual abuse media?

_____

_____

_____

3. What "defense strategy" did your "inner attorney" use that allowed you to continue using child sexual abuse media?

_____

_____

_____

4. Can you take responsibility for your "inner attorney? and his/her behaviors? Do you manage your "inner attorney"? If yes, explain how you manage him/her.

_____

_____

_____

5. How can your therapist(s) and/or group support you in managing your "inner attorney"?

_____

_____

_____

_____

React

One thing that is often helpful when managing your "inner attorney" is to find a physical, visual representation of your "inner attorney." When working with clients, we use a toy action figure from the movie *Men in Black* that looks like an attorney. However, you are free to find any representation that helps to remind you of when your "inner attorney" is present.

Notes

_____

_____

_____

_____

_____

_____

_____

_____

_____

_____

The Change Process

It's been said, *"The only thing constant is change."* Learning to do something differently is not an easy task. People get comfortable with their way of thinking, feeling, and behaving and it is hard to do things differently. If we must change, then it is important to think about how change actually happens.

In the early 1970's, researchers studied ways to help people change their cigarette smoking habits. They noticed the same patterns across multiple people as they each moved through the change process. The researchers focused on mapping out the change process so others would benefit from understanding how to make changes in their own lives and by making those changes long-lasting.

Below is the roadmap the researchers made about how people change:

Stages of Change

Illustration based on the Stages of Change proposed by Prochaska, J. O., & DiClemente, C. C. (1983)

1) Pre-Contemplation

People in this stage are not aware or willing to admit they have a problem. You'll notice in the graphic above that the figure is missing their head. This represents the fact that they have not even thought about change yet. More often than not, they are in denial about the change that needs to occur. Even when faced with a mountain of evidence about their problem, they cannot see a need for change.

2) Contemplation

There is a sense of ambivalence at this stage. Sometimes, you think you might have a problem, and other times, you think you don't have a problem. Perhaps you begin thinking about the costs/benefits if you were to make a change. You may be considering the consequences you have experienced as evidence that you need to change. You may begin hearing the voices of others who have said to you, "There is something wrong." In any case, you are starting to consider the fact that change may be on the horizon, even though you are not necessarily ready for it.

3) Preparation

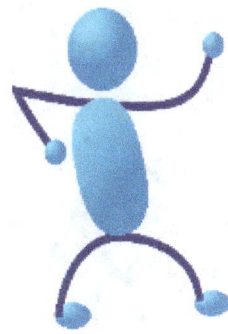

During this stage, you have moved beyond your ambivalence and are beginning to accept that change is necessary. Whether you plan to make this change to benefit you personally, to satisfy others in your life, or to avoid consequences (including legal consequences) – you have decided to make a change.

4) Action

Now comes the giant leap… taking action based on your preparation. Maybe in the previous stage you looked up the information for a recovery group. In this stage, you actually attend the group. Perhaps you found a book to read (or bought this workbook), but instead letting it sit on your shelf, you now pick it up and begin to read it.

Think of this stage as the moment after a movie director sets up a scene, and yells, "ACTION!" All the moving parts start working together towards creating new ways of thinking, feeling, and behaving.

5) Maintenance

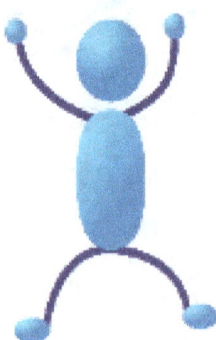

You're arrived! Or have you? This stage involves keeping the change within range so you can continue to perform maintenance. Let's say the engine blows up in your car and you pay the money to fix it. On the way out the door, the mechanic says, *"Try and remember to change the oil this time."* In this stage, you must remember to change the oil and do the required maintenance so that the change becomes more long-term rather than short-lived.

6) Recycle (Lapse/Relapse)

There is a difference between lapsing and relapsing. In the case of this workbook, a relapse would be crossing a boundary by viewing child sexual abuse media or exploiting a child in another way. However, a lapse might be less severe – perhaps you saw an advertisement on television and sexualized a child in the commercial. You haven't really crossed into a relapse YET, but it still counts as a lapse.

When you lapse you can recycle as the change process suggests. Following a lapse, you re-enter the change process and use the new information you've gained to make the change more solid and long-lasting. Recycling and lapsing are not failures but rather opportunities to make changes even more permanent.

Why it is possible to recycle a relapse, these more serious behaviors take more work to recycle and typically have additional consequences associated with them.

Reflect & Respond

1. What stage do you think you are in currently now that you are working on changing your use of child sexual abuse media?

   _____

   _____

   _____

2. Make a list below of at least five reasons why you want to change your viewing of child sexual abuse media (e.g., legal trouble, anxiety about getting caught, relationship issues, etc.). Circle the one or two that are most motivating for you.

   _____

   _____

   _____

3. Many times, we are ready for change when we are in crisis or chaos. If that is true for you, when the dust settles, what can be your backup source of motivation for changing your viewing of child sexual abuse media?

   _____

   _____

   _____

   _____

4. Imagine yourself moving through the stages of change. How would your thinking, feeling, and actions look different than what they are right now?

_____

_____

_____

5. Write in the space below ONE thought you are willing to change or ONE action you are willing to take that would propel you towards your next stage of change.

_____

_____

_____

_____

_____

_____

React

Find one trusted person in your life who knows your story (most of it, anyway) that could review this worksheet with you. Make your case for your perception of your current stage of change.

Do they agree with you? Do they see you in the same stage? Do they have any feedback for you? Do they believe you can make the one change you listed in #5 above? How can you use their support in moving through the stages of change regarding your problematic online sexual behavior, including your use of child sexual abuse media?

Notes

_____

_____

_____

_____

_____

_____

_____

_____

_____

_____

_____

_____

_____

_____

_____

The Seven Desires

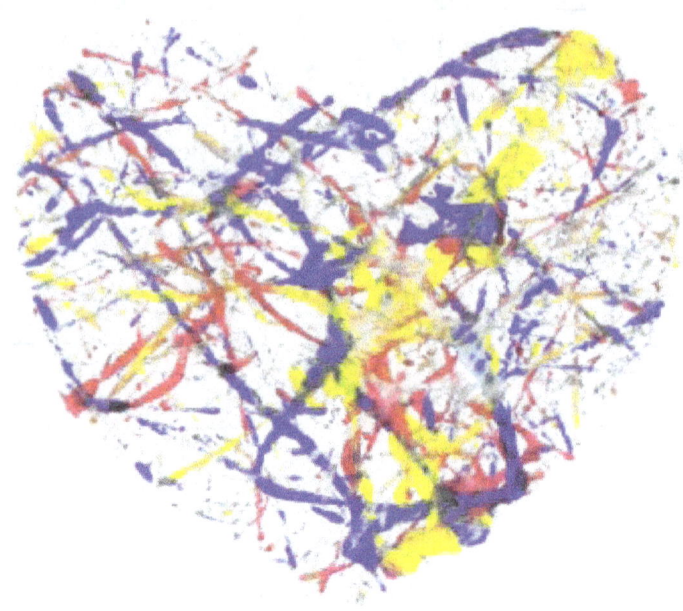

Regardless of our age, gender, ethnic background, or culture, the Seven Desires are universal. These Seven Desires are not new. They have been discussed in many ways for many years. However, we like how Mark and Debbie Laaser describe the Seven Desires.

1) To Be Heard and Understood

We all want our words to be heard and understood, but we also want people in our lives to hear and understand us as a human being. Sometimes, when we don't feel *heard*, we talk louder, repeat ourselves over and over again, or become defensive and argumentative. When we don't feel *understood* – we may revert back to a child or rebellious teenager. We scream, plead, stomp, hit, or throw a temper tantrum either emotionally or sometimes even physically. We can also "act in" instead of acting out, becoming depressed, suicidal, or desperate just to be heard and understood.

2)   To Be Affirmed

We all desire to have friends and others who recognize and acknowledge what we think, feel, and do. Some of us grew up in families or environments that not only failed to affirm us but actively criticized us for our thoughts, feelings, and behaviors. If you did not get affirmation as a child and/or were actively criticized, you may avoid people you fear will repeat this pattern. Some people try to overcome this lack of affirmation by always seeking the approval of others, no matter what is asked of them. Others may turn to their sexuality as a way to be affirmed by others.

3)   To Be Blessed

While affirmations are about what we do, blessings are about who we are. The blessing comes from not doing anything but being who we are and allowing others to love us. When we don't feel blessed by others, we may feel shame - as if we are a "mistake." Those who were not blessed as children often go through life angry or sad.

4)   To Be Safe

While physical safety is an obvious desire, we also desire to be emotionally safe. We want people around us who are reliable and can be counted on to protect us both physically and emotionally. A lack of physical or emotional safety results in high levels of anxiety. People who lack safety often look "crazy" to others. Their anxiety leaks out everywhere and affects their relationship with themselves and those around them. When we don't feel safe in life, we often have difficulty trusting ourselves and others.

5)   To Be Touched

The desire to be touched can be about physical or sexual touch, but it can also refer to being touched emotionally or spiritually. We never outgrow the need to be touched. Touch releases powerful "feel good" chemicals in our brains. Being touched by others helps us know we are loved and cared for by them. If we didn't get enough touch in our lives when we were infants and children, then we often end up with a lifelong hunger for touch. We may turn to impersonal or inappropriate online sexuality to get these "touch needs" met.

6)   To Be Chosen

It is a beautiful experience to be chosen! We feel chosen in romantic relationships. We feel chosen in friendships. We feel chosen when someone asks us for help. We feel chosen when we receive praise at work. We all love being chosen. Being chosen means we are special and accepted. When our desire to be chosen is lacking, we feel unlovable or feel that we are never quite good enough. The result is often feelings of loneliness, despair, and hopelessness.

7)   To Be Included

The desire to be included is about belonging in community with others. We all long to be part of something bigger than ourselves. It helps us feel like we are not alone. Belonging has all types of emotional, physical, and spiritual benefits. When we don't feel included, we can become desperate to be included. People who feel like outcasts will often ignore their morals, values, and beliefs just to be included in a group.

Impact of the Seven Desires

We all long for the Seven Desires to be met in our lives. When the Seven Desires are unmet in childhood or adulthood, it can result in negative feelings, beliefs, and behaviors. Unfulfilled longing for the Seven Desires begins a chain of negativity that often results in unhealthy coping strategies and behaviors. When we are unable to get our Seven Desires met in healthy ways, we often turn to unhealthy coping strategies such as alcohol, drugs, overeating, shopping, gambling, and sex. These unhealthy coping strategies, including the viewing of child sexual abuse media, provide a brief relief from our discomfort and a false sense that one of our desires is being met.

7 Desires of the Heart

(Developed by Deb and Mark Laaser)

 1. To be heard and understood.

 2. To be affirmed.

 3. To be blessed.

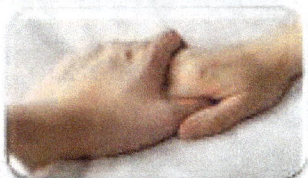 4. To be touched.

 5. To be safe.

 6. To be chosen.

 7. To be included.

Reflect & Respond

1.   Which of the Seven Desires did you get met by family and/or others in childhood? Specifically, note the person who met your Seven Desires as a child.

   _____

   _____

   _____

2.   Which of the Seven Desires were not met by your family or others in childhood?

   _____

   _____

   _____

3.   Which of the Seven Desires are met or not met in your current relationships with partners, family, and friends?

   _____

   _____

   _____

4.   Do you think a longing for one or more of the Seven Desires played a role in your use of child sexual abuse media?

   _____

   _____

   _____

React

On the following page, you will see a graphic called the Seven Desires Iceberg. The graphic illustrates that while viewing child sexual abuse media is often a "surface level" issue, it is an underlying Seven Desires that must be addressed for the problematic online sexual behavior to stop. In particular, noting which of the Seven Desires you long for the most and have the most difficulty getting met in your life is the first step in addressing your use of child sexual abuse media.

On the iceberg, take a pencil and circle the top three desires that you believe you long for the most and have the most difficulty meeting in your life. Reflect on how the lack of these three desires may have contributed to your use of child sexual abuse media. Don't use this exercise to make excuses for your behavior but rather use it to understand better what's below the surface of YOUR iceberg.

Next, on the iceberg illustration near each of the Seven Desires, there is a blank space. With a _pencil_, rank order your Seven Desires by writing a number, 1 through 7, in the blank space. Label the desire you lack the most in life as #1… then the second desire, and so on until you have rank-ordered all Seven Desires.

As you progress throughout the workbook, you will continue to learn more about the Seven Desires, yourself, and your online sexual behavior. You may need to revisit this illustration and re-rank these Seven Desires to match your newfound self-awareness.

Notes

_____

_____

_____

_____

_____

The Seven Desires Iceberg

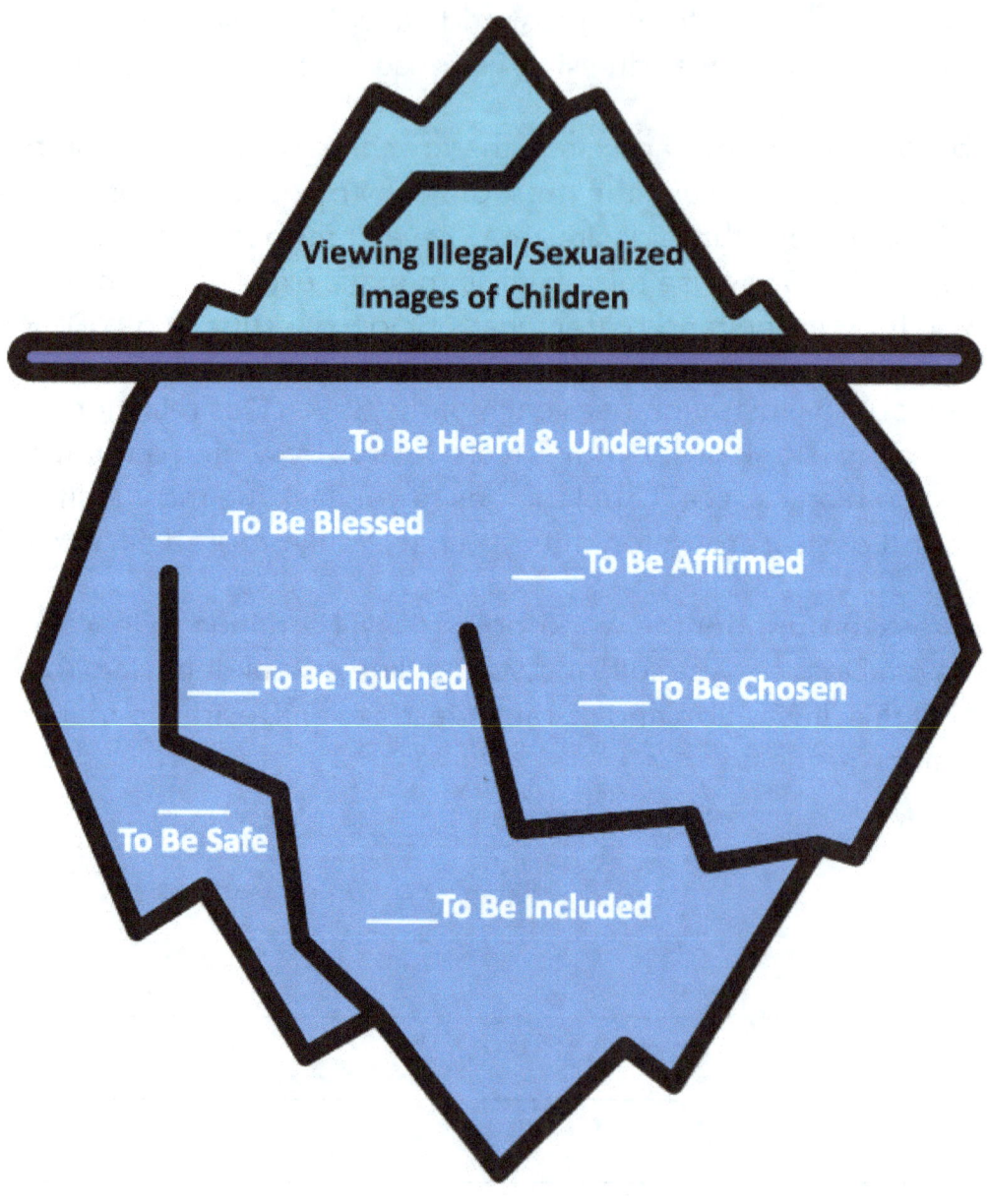

Viewing Illegal/Sexualized Images of Children

_____To Be Heard & Understood

_____To Be Blessed

_____To Be Affirmed

_____To Be Touched

_____To Be Chosen

_____
To Be Safe

_____To Be Included

The Inner Warrior

Everyone needs an Inner Warrior to help them fight life's battles! This is especially true for those battling difficult issues within themselves (e.g., viewing child sexual abuse media). An Inner Warrior helps you take the next right steps when you are uncertain.

When you visualize your Inner Warrior, what do they look like? He/she may (or may not) look like the warriors on this page, however how he/she looks is not what matters – what matters is what your Inner Warrior can do for you.

There will be times while doing the exercises in this workbook that you feel overwhelmed, hopeless, or defeated, but conjuring up your Inner Warrior can help you stay the course and continue moving forward in addressing your online sexual offense behavior.

What can your Inner Warrior Do for you?

Fight for your values and morals when it gets difficult for you.

Provide you with inner strength when life gets hard.

Provide resilience when you get knocked down.

Pick you back up and get you on track.

Help you stay the course when you feel like giving up.

Believe in you when you cannot find the confidence to believe in yourself.

Reflect & Respond

1. What does your Inner Warrior look like? What are his/her characteristics? His/her strengths?

_____

_____

_____

2. Does he/she remind you of any real-life people you know? A family member, friend, mentor?

_____

_____

_____

3. What warning signs in your body/mind would indicate you need to call on your Inner Warrior for help?

_____

_____

_____

React

To remember that you have an Inner Warrior, you need a visual representation of him/her. If you are artistic, draw a picture of him/her. If you're not, find a picture of him/her online (if you have access). You may even want to purchase a visual representation of something that can represent your Inner Warrior.

If none of these options work, simply write down words on a piece of paper that represent the characteristics and strengths you need in an Inner Warrior. Place the visual representation nearby so you'll remember what you need from him/her when the time arises.

Notes

_____

_____

_____

_____

_____

_____

Hermes' Web

Hermes' Web is a colorful, hands-on tool that can help you identify and address issues and concerns in your life. In this workbook, Hermes' Web is used to identify the six core issues that often underlie the use of child sexual abuse media.

This isn't the only way to use Hermes' Web, but using it in this way to increase your awareness about these issues will help you throughout the remainder of the workbook.

We have taken some liberties in simplifying Hermes' Web and distilling it down to its main concepts for this exercise. Below is some basic information and a graphic that will be useful.

There are several "spokes" around Hermes' Web. The top of the yellow spoke represents the "public self" – a part of ourselves that we shine up to show the rest of the world. We all need a public self, or we would be a mess out in the world. There is a black barrier on the yellow spoke, and below this barrier represents the private self. Individuals tend to "stuff" their problems beneath the barrier over time instead of dealing with them directly. We tell ourselves, "We will solve those problems later," but we often never do, building up pressure in the private self.

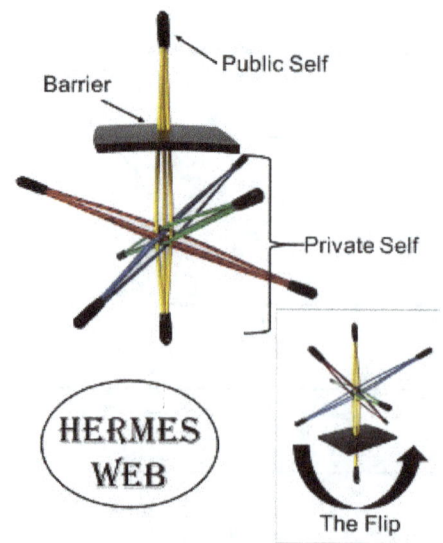

When the "pressure" below the barrier in the private self becomes too much, individuals tend to "flip." During the "flip," the private self comes to the surface while the public self goes underneath. When your private self "flips" to the surface, all the issues you tried to keep hidden beneath the barrier are exposed, and you "act out."

Common examples of acting out include excessive alcohol or drug use, raging at others, binge eating, using child sexual abuse media, etc. After the "flip," you "flip back" and put your public self on top to begin shining it up again with the hope that you will never "flip" again.

There are six common issues that individuals involved with using child sexual abuse media typically "stuff" beneath their barrier. There are likely more than six, but these are the most common. And, while you may not struggle with all six, you most likely struggle with more than one.

The six most common issues are listed below:

- Poor Emotion Management – typically negative emotions such as depression, anxiety, anger, loneliness, boredom, etc.
- Inadequate Intimacy Skills – poor interpersonal skills and difficulty building relationships
- Deviant Sexuality: Sexual interest - arousal in prepubescent/pubescent children
- Out of Control Sexual Behavior – a sense that you have lost control of when you start or stop your sexual behavior (some people refer to this as hypersexuality, sexual preoccupation, using sex to cope, and/or sexual addiction)
- Problematic Technology Use – not understanding the psychology of technology and using technology to manage your negative emotions
- Lack of Victim Awareness – not understanding the impact of child sexual abuse media on victims

Look at the second illustration of Hermes' Web to see these six areas labeled.

When you stuff these issues below your barrier and the pressure builds, the resulting "flip" can often result in the use of child sexual abuse media.

HERMES WEB

Public Self

Barrier

1

2

3

6

5

4

1. Poor Emotional Management
2. Inadequate Relationship/Intimacy Skills
3. Out of Control Sexual Behavior
4. Deviant Sexual Interest
5. Problematic Technology Use
6. Lack of Victim Awareness

Reflect & Respond

1. Now that you have learned about Hermes' Web and the common core problems of individuals who view child sexual abuse media, which of these six core problems do you believe are most problematic for you? You may select one, two, three, four, five, or all six… it's up to you. Order your core problems from most problematic to least problematic. Your answers may change as you progress through the workbook, and that's ok!

_____

_____

_____

We recommend going through the entire workbook even though you may not believe all of the six core issues apply to you. Believe us when we say that each chapter will have information for you that will be helpful in your goal of not using child sexual abuse media.

React

Explain the Hermes' Web process to your partner, a family member, or a close friend. You can use any type of behavior; however, if you have a therapist or are part of a therapy group, explain your use of child sexual abuse media using Hermes' Web.

** If you would like to purchase a Hermes' Web you can go to www.hermesweb.com. **Enter the code HWEB20** to receive a 20% discount on a 6-inch or 8-inch Herme's Web.

Notes

_____

_____

_____

_____

_____

_____

_____

_____

Chapter 2: Emotion Management

The inability to manage emotions is at the "heart" of many psychological issues, including the use of child sexual abuse media. Learning to manage your emotions in healthy and positive ways is a crucial skill to moving away from unhealthy sexual behavior and moving toward healthy sexual behavior.

This chapter will provide exercises to help you better understand and manage your emotions. The hope is that these new skills will assist you in breaking the cycle of turning to the online world of sexuality as a place to "soothe and calm" your negative emotions.

A List of Chapter Exercises

1. Emotional Awareness
2. Getting to Know Your Inner Critters
3. EQ Barometer
4. A Wise Mind
5. Emotional Banking
6. The Emotional Regulator
7. Mindfulness

Don't Forget!

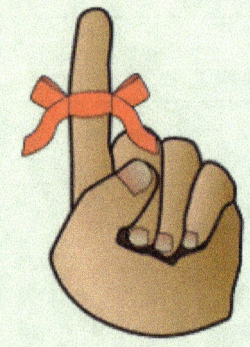

Those who have access to the Internet may want to visit our companion website for resources related to this and other chapters in the workbook. These resources include additional articles, websites, and copies of activities/graphics from the chapters.

http://www.internetbehavior.com/illegalimages

Emotional Awareness

"How does that make you feel?"

It's such a simple question, but it baffles even the best of us. Many people can't identify their feelings. Why is this? It's hard to say. Some grew up in environments where their feelings didn't matter, often being dismissed or outright ignored by those around them. For others, emotions are scary because they have seen the people close to them lose control when confronted with their feelings. Maybe Dad raged when he was angry, maybe Mom threatened to kill herself when she was sad. Maybe Aunt Martha drank her way through her emotions, and even though Uncle Bill always looked happy, behind closed doors he took his resentment out on his wife. You get the idea... if emotions are so scary, maybe it's best just to ignore them?

Here's the rub. Ignoring emotions doesn't mean you don't have them. They are always there... deep under the surface... and they affect you every day. Not naming them isn't helpful; in fact, it's like having a disease that doctors can't diagnose. It's nerve-wracking! And while being unable to name the emotions you are experiencing can certainly be nerve-wracking for you, it is most definitely nerve-wracking for others.

"My partner says I don't love them, but I really do," or *"I don't know why I was viewing child pornography, it just happened."* These are just a couple of examples of how unnamed feelings can look when they are ignored, minimized, or denied.

At the most basic level, there are four core emotions: happiness, anger, fear, and sadness. These four then begin to divide and combine to create other, more nuanced emotions, but let's start with the basics.

THE FOUR CORE EMOTIONS

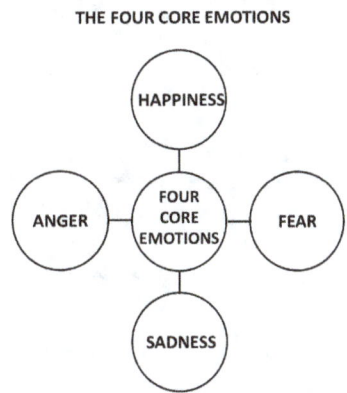

Stop what you are doing right now and see if you can identify which of these four basic feelings you are currently experiencing. It doesn't have to be only one. Emotions are complex, and you may very well be experiencing more than one at a time.

If you are struggling, let's try this. Your body is often the truth-teller of emotions. Do a "body scan." Close your eyes and start focusing on your body from top to bottom. Slowly, beginning with your face and head, start cataloguing your feelings and sensations, eventually moving lower to your shoulders and chest. After that, go even lower to your stomach and hips, before finally directing your focus down through your legs to your feet. It's a bit like playing "Head, Shoulders, Knees and Toes" when you were a kid. Pay attention to any subtle body sensations you are feeling. Pain. Tension. Itchiness. Numbness. Coldness. What do you think your body is trying to tell you about your emotions? Tension = Anger. Fast Heartbeat = Fear. Sighs = Sadness. Relaxed Jaw = Happy. Can you feel it? Can you translate it?

Sometimes people say, *"I know I'm feeling something, but I can't name what it is."* When this is the case, a feelings chart might be useful. There are hundreds out there, but we have included the one on the previous page to get you started.

Like everything else, it takes practice to identify emotions. Use this chart to help you start naming your emotions. If you have access to the Internet, look at other feelings charts to start naming even more emotions than just the ones listed here. Stop several times a day and ask yourself, "How am I feeling?" Do a body scan and let your body help you identify the feelings that may be hiding from you.

One suggestion to help to name your emotions is to forget the word "like" whenever you're talking about your feelings. If you find yourself saying *"I feel like…,"* instead try eliminating the word "like" from the sentence and just say *"I feel…."* Rewrite the following "I feel like" statements.

I feel like I should go to bed.   I feel _____

I feel like no one does their job at work.   I feel _____

I feel like I'm getting sick.   I feel _____

I feel like the party will be fun.   I feel _____

I feel like this class is hard.   I feel _____

Reflect & Respond

1. Recognizing feelings isn't easy. Many people never get beyond the four basic emotions, but it's important that you keep trying. You would be surprised at how helpful it will be to develop a "feelings language" to better understand yourself and express your feelings to others. While looking at the large feelings chart above, find and list five feelings (beyond the four basic ones) that you experience in a week.

    _____

    _____

    _____

2. Spend the day listening to what others have to say and observing their non-verbal communication. Can you name some of the feelings you think they may have been experiencing? Correctly naming another person's feelings is good practice for both empathy and emotion identification.

_____

_____

_____

3. What feelings have you "stuffed" – ignored, minimized, or denied – and how do you think that stuffing of your feelings may have contributed to your viewing of child sexual abuse media?

_____

_____

_____

React

Make a copy of the Feelings Chart at the end of this exercise or print a copy of the Feelings Chart from the workbook's companion website: www.internetbehavior.com/illegalimages.

Hang your Feelings Chart in a place you will see every morning so you can place a "marker" on the strongest feeling for you that morning. You can use a magnet on the fridge, a gemstone on your desk, etc., as your marker. Before you go to bed at night, move the "marker" to your new strongest emotion (or leave it alone if the emotion hasn't changed for the day). Do this for at least one week to help you identify your emotions and see how they change (or don't) over the course of each day.

Extra Credit: Watch the movie "Inside Out" and/or "Inside Out 2." It is an animated children's movie about emotions, but it certainly applies to adults who also struggle with identifying their emotions. Write some thoughts about what you learned about feelings while watching the movie.

Notes

_____

_____

_____

_____

_____

_____

_____

_____

_____

_____

_____

_____

_____

_____

_____

Getting to Know Your Inner Critters

We all have inner critters that represent our emotional lives. Elizabeth, for example, is always working to manage her anxiety and often looks like an anxious bunny running from one thing to another. When she gets overwhelmed, she often turns into a turtle hiding out inside her shell. For David, when he feels ornery and contrary, he turns into a raccoon, causing all sorts of trouble for everyone. When he gets angry, he can turn into a grizzly bear, loud and bellowing.

Our inner critters are not good or bad; they just are. Going into a turtle's shell and having a day of isolation can be therapeutic, but staying there for weeks and weeks becomes problematic. Getting angry and occasionally softly "growling" at others is not a big deal; however, standing on your hind legs, looking threatening, and growling loudly at others is not okay.

The trick is to recognize your inner critters and learn skills to manage them when they get "out of control" and become problematic for yourself and others in your lives.

Other examples of inner critters:

Porcupine - sarcastic, prickly, assertive
Koala Bear - zoned out, out of touch, relaxed
Shark - aggressive, violent, protective

Reflect & Respond

1. Think of the people that you know and see if you can identify their inner critters.

_____

_____

_____

2. Identify some of your inner critters. What emotion does each critter represent?

_____

_____

_____

3. What inner critters at least partially facilitated your viewing of child sexual abuse media? What skills do you have (if any) to manage that critter in the future? No worries if you feel like your critter management skills are lacking; the last three exercises in this chapter are designed to assist with skill management.

_____

_____

_____

React

Search for visual representations of your inner critters. It could be a photo, a stuffed animal, a small cage, etc. Use this visualization to remind you of when your emotional critter needs management.

List here what you found as your visualizations:

_____

_____

_____

ELIZABETH

DAVID

EQ Barometer

Do you know what IQ is? It stands for your Intelligence Quotient. By definition, most people in the world have average intelligence. That's what "average" means! Others struggle with intellectual disabilities, while another group is highly intelligent. But there is another type of intelligence that is far more important than IQ when it comes to addressing your use of child sexual abuse media. After all, you probably knew it was illegal and would cause you problems in your life. Your IQ was just fine. It was your EQ that was lacking.

What is *EQ*? EQ stands for Emotional Quotient or Emotional Intelligence. EQ is the ability to recognize, understand, and manage your emotions both when things are going well and when you are triggered, and life is not going your way. Those with poor EQ take out their emotions (e.g., frustration, anger, anxiety, etc.) on others, while those with high EQ learn to manage their emotions and use certain techniques to avoid causing harm to self and others.

EQ has two levels: basic EQ and EQ 2.0. Basic EQ focuses on your own self-awareness and on managing your own emotions and behaviors. That is to say, it helps you recognize your own emotions and understand the impact they have in your life. Additionally, you can apply basic EQ skills to manage and control your emotions in healthy ways.

EQ 2.0 uses the same skills from the level of basic EQ, but rather than applying them to yourself, you now begin applying those skills to others. EQ 2.0 requires you to understand the emotions, needs, and concerns of others. With EQ 2.0, you can decipher emotional cues and respond to social situations appropriately. You are mature, confident, and comfortable around others. Furthermore, you can manage your emotions with others even when life sucks. When operating on the level of EQ 2.0, you are aware of the impact you have on others, and you can develop and maintain good relationships for the long-haul.

Remember the story of the guy who kicks his dog when he gets home from work because he had a bad day? That's an example of poor EQ. The man in the story can't manage his emotions, so he acts out and harms another living being. You might think that's terrible, but isn't that exactly what was happening whenever you viewed child sexual abuse media? You used images that victimized children to satisfy your own emotional and sexual needs – it was your version of kicking the dog.

The good news is that it's never too late to develop Emotional Intelligence. To get you started, take a look at the following list of 10 things you can do to help you develop EQ and EQ 2.0.

- Name and talk about your feelings.
- Don't avoid your emotions.
- Know your emotional triggers - who and what can set you off?
- Keep a journal about your emotions.
- Don't always trust your emotions - they may be tricking you.
- Try to "even out" your emotions - the lows and highs will pass.
- Stop, ask yourself why you are feeling what you feel in the moment.
- Spot emotions in books, movies, television, etc.
- Seek feedback from others about your emotional responses.
- Know the impact your emotions have on others.

Reflect & Respond

1. What would others say about your Emotional Intelligence? What would your family and friends say about your EQ/EQ2.0? What about your boss or co-workers? What about the person in front of you in a long line at the grocery store? What would your pets say?

_____

_____

_____

_____

_____

_____

2. Now that you know more about EQ and EQ 2.0, list five additional actions you can take to help build EQ/EQ 2.0.

_____

_____

_____

Notes

_____

_____

_____

_____

_____

_____

_____

_____

_____

_____

_____

React

Pretend your EQ can be measured. A barometer is a device that measures atmospheric pressure, and it can be helpful in predicting future weather events based on its readings. What is the barometer that can help you monitor your EQ? If you can imagine that the ways you think, feel, and behave are indicative of pressure building inside you, then you can use an EQ barometer to predict your future interactions with yourself and others.

For example, when I begin to curse more frequently and start using *F* bombs in all my conversations, it means my pressure is building and I need to pause and take an EQ inventory of myself. I need to stop and use those 10 tips listed above.

One client said his barometer of EQ is when he begins to overeat. Another yells at his kids more often. Another becomes extremely sarcastic. Another becomes passive aggressive with others.

Think about your barometer – or the measure of pressure in your life that causes your EQ to diminish and leads to negative behaviors. You may even notice that the temptation to view child sexual abuse media increases in direct proportion to how much pressure builds on your barometer.

On the picture of the barometer below, write words or draw pictures of three to five things which indicate that your "pressure" is building and that you need to pause and visit your EQ tools to prevent the storm from coming. Don't worry if you can't think of these tools right now, since we will address them in other exercises in this chapter.

Links to these books that can help you with understanding EQ and developing EQ tools can be found on the workbook's companion website, www.internetbehavior.com/illegalimages.

Emotional Intelligence 2.0 by Travis Bradberry
Emotional Intelligence Habits by Travis Bradberry

My EQ Barometer

A Wise Mind

I'm sure you know that your brain is divided into various parts, such as the left hemisphere, the right hemisphere, the prefrontal cortex, and the amygdala. But did you know that your **mind** is also divided into multiple parts? This exercise will introduce you to the three main parts of your mind and how each one can impact your emotional regulation, both positively and negatively.

Take a look at the illustration in this exercise and refer to it as you read the descriptions of the different types of minds.

The first part of your mind is the **"emotional mind."** This is where you **feel** things. Some people are very in touch with this part of their mind, and we often refer to them as "emotional people." Others may not have connected with their emotional mind in years. It is important to remember that emotions simply exist—they are not necessarily good or bad. However, you need the other parts of your mind to help you react to your emotions appropriately. When the emotional mind acts on its own, it is often impulsive, unrestrained, and sometimes even chaotic.

The second part of your mind is the **"logical mind."** This is the part that **thinks** about things. It helps with problem-solving and logical reasoning. There are times when your logical mind must take over. For example, consider an airline pilot in a critical situation while flying a plane. If you were a passenger on that plane, you would want the pilot's logical mind to be in control—making decisions, developing solutions, and ensuring a safe landing. However, in everyday situations, relying solely on your logical mind can be problematic. If you approach problems purely with logic and ignore your own emotions or the feelings of others, you may find yourself in difficult situations (and we're not talking about a relaxing jacuzzi!).

Finally, we have the **"wise mind."** The wise mind serves as an intermediary between your emotional mind and your logical mind. It helps maintain a balance between the two and plays a crucial role in emotional regulation. While each of these minds has its strengths and weaknesses, daily life typically requires all three to function effectively. Without your wise mind to mediate between your emotional and logical minds, you might experience strained relationships, emotional distress, and other negative consequences. In other words, your emotional regulation depends on your wise mind.

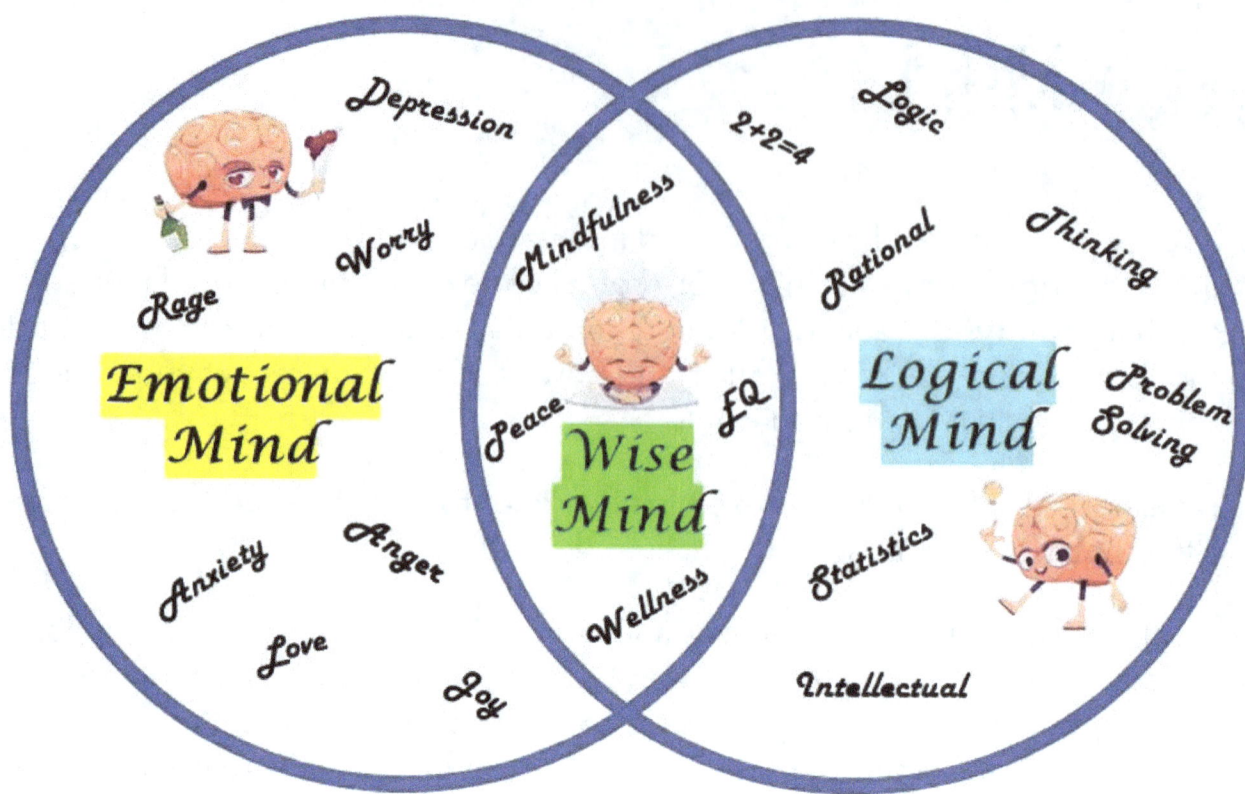

Reflect & Respond

1. As you think about your "three minds," how do you think each of these has been helpful or harmful to you in your life?

    _____

    _____

    _____

2. Remember back to a situation where you had an argument or disagreement with someone. It could be a family member, a co-worker, your boss, a probation officer, a friend, etc. How could your wise mind have helped you in this situation?

    _____

    _____

    _____

3. In Chapter 1, "Building the Foundations," we had you identify and visualize your "Inner Warrior." Remember him/her? How do you think your Inner Warrior and your wise mind can work together to help with your emotional regulation?

_____

_____

_____

React

The decision to view child sexual abuse media requires that you ignore your wise mind. What happened to your wise mind when you were viewing these images and videos? Which mind hijacked your behavior? Was it a desperate need to fulfill one of the Seven Desires? Was it sexual excitement?

Other chapters of this book will guide you through developing your wise mind, but what are some of your current ideas on how your wise mind can be included in your future decision-making, especially about child sexual abuse media?

Learning to invite your wise mind to take part in your life is an important step in helping to regulate your emotional and logical minds. When we are not balanced and wise, we risk becoming unregulated. Invite your wise mind into situations where you need help with your emotional regulation and then record your results.

_____

_____

_____

_____

_____

Emotional Banking

Emotional Banking is the practice of consciously deciding how you earn, spend, and save your Emotional Units (EUs). EUs are difficult to earn yet incredibly easy to spend. Earning EUs requires deliberate thought and action, whereas spending them often happens without a second thought. In fact, EUs can disappear in a nanosecond.

Consider how you spend EUs each day. Do you get frustrated during your commute to work? That's at least 25 EUs gone. Do you start your day feeling stressed about everything you need to accomplish? There go another 50 EUs. Do you rush through your day feeling overwhelmed and depleted? More EUs vanish. If you're like most people, you likely end the day having spent more EUs than you have in your Emotional Bank Account.

Now, think about how you earn EUs. Do you take a few moments throughout the day to breathe and de-stress? Do you make time for a nutritious lunch? Do you step away from work for a short walk to clear your mind? Do you go to therapy on a regular basis? Do you connect with people in your support system? These are examples of EU deposits. If you're like most people, you may not prioritize these deposits in your daily and weekly routine.

If our assumptions are correct, you likely spend more EUs than you have each day and fail to make consistent or substantial deposits into your Emotional Bank Account.

When you live in a constant state of emotional overdraft—spending more EUs than you have—you become more susceptible to unhealthy coping behaviors.

Taking care of yourself emotionally means being mindful of your EUs. On average, we receive about 500 EUs per day. To illustrate this concept, let's take a look at "Bob's" Emotional Bank Account below.

BOB's EMOTIONAL BANK ACCOUNT

	Emotional Units (EUs)
Line 1. Starting Balance (carry over from yesterday)	0
Line 2. Starting Balance Today	500
Line 3. Daily Checking Deposits (positive, healthy behaviors/activities) Took a walk at lunch at work	50
Line 4. (Add Line1, Line 2, and all your deposits from Line 3) Total EUs	550
Line 5. Daily Checking Withdraws (negative, unhealthy behaviors/activities) Went to bed late – tired and sluggish today	100
Stressful day at work, not managing anxiety well	150
Did not connect with friends/family today - isolating	50
Watched adult porn – turned into child sexual abuse material	350
Went to bed late again – feeling tired and disgusted with self	50
Line 6. (Add all withdraws from Line 6) Total EU Withdraws	700
Line 7. Line 4 minus Line 6 (may be a negative number)	- 150
Line 8. If Line 7. is a positive number, enter here and transfer to Line 1. of tomorrow's blank EUs sheet.	
Line 9. If Line 7. Is negative, you need to strategize on building your EUs. Tomorrow's a New Day! Enter 0 here and transfer to Line 1. on tomorrow's blank EUs sheet.	0

Reflect & Respond

1. What is your initial reaction to the idea of earning, spending, and saving EUs?

   _____

   _____

   _____

2. Are you a careful saver of your EUs or do you spend your EUs recklessly?

   _____

   _____

   _____

3. What do you typically spend EUs on each day? Do you typically spend EUs on insignificant or unimportant things? If so, provide some examples.

   _____

   _____

   _____

4. Do you make any daily EU deposits into your Emotional Bank Account

   _____

   _____

   _____

5. List five things that you can do daily to contribute to your Emotional Bank Account.

_____

_____

_____

React

Make 14 copies of the Emotional Bank Account sheet on the following page. Then, complete the Emotional Bank Account sheets based on your daily activities. You can also find a blank copy of the Emotional Bank Account sheet on the workbook's companion website: www.internetbehavior.com/ illegalimages.

You will determine exactly how many Emotional Units (EUs) to assign to each thought, emotion, and behavior. In Bob's example, he viewed child sexual abuse media and determined that this action resulted in a withdrawal of 350 EUs. Earlier that day, he went for a walk and decided that activity was worth a deposit of 50 EUs.

These numbers are somewhat subjective, as you will assign their value yourself. On a day when you really need to take a walk, you might determine that it's worth 75 EUs instead of 50 EUs. Try to base the value of each activity on an accurate estimation of its intensity and impact on your life. Remember, if the values for your activities aren't accurate, you are only deceiving yourself!

After the first week, carefully review your tracking sheets. What patterns do you notice in terms of deposits and withdrawals? Do you consistently make the same withdrawals? Are there certain days of the week or particular events that impact your Emotional Bank Account balance?

On days when you were low on EUs or emptied your account, were you more tempted to view child sexual abuse media? Think back to when you engaged in this behavior—what would your balance sheet have looked like on those days?

EMOTIONAL BANK ACCOUNT

	Emotional Units (EUs)
Line 1. Starting Balance (carry over from yesterday)	
Line 2. Starting Balance Today	500
Line 3. Daily Checking Deposits (positive, healthy behaviors/activities) _____ _____ _____ _____ _____	 _____ _____ _____ _____ _____
Line 4. **(Add Line1, Line 2, and all your deposits from Line 3) Total EUs**	
Line 5. Daily Checking Withdraws (negative, unhealthy behaviors/activities) _____ _____ _____ _____ _____	 _____ _____ _____ _____ _____
Line 6. **(Add all withdraws from Line 6) Total EU Withdraws**	
Line 7. **Line 4 minus Line 6 (may be a negative number)**	
Line 8. **If Line 7. is a positive number, enter here and transfer to Line 1. of tomorrow's blank EUs sheet.**	
Line 9. **If Line 7. Is negative, you need to strategize on building your EUs. Tomorrow's a New Day! Enter 0 here and transfer to Line 1. on tomorrow's blank EUs sheet.**	

EMOTIONAL BANK ACCOUNT

	Emotional Units (EUs)
Line 1. Starting Balance (carry over from yesterday)	
Line 2. Starting Balance Today	500
Line 3. Daily Checking Deposits (positive, healthy behaviors/activities) _____ _____ _____ _____ _____	_____ _____ _____ _____ _____
Line 4. (Add Line1, Line 2, and all your deposits from Line 3) Total EUs	
Line 5. Daily Checking Withdraws (negative, unhealthy behaviors/activities) _____ _____ _____ _____ _____	_____ _____ _____ _____ _____
Line 6. (Add all withdraws from Line 6) Total EU Withdraws	
Line 7. Line 4 minus Line 6 (may be a negative number)	
Line 8. If Line 7. is a positive number, enter here and transfer to Line 1. of tomorrow's blank EUs sheet.	
Line 9. If Line 7. Is negative, you need to strategize on building your EUs. Tomorrow's a New Day! Enter 0 here and transfer to Line 1. on tomorrow's blank EUs sheet.	

The Emotional Regulator

There are websites online where people post images of odd, unusual, or unexpected things, and then visitors to the site are invited to guess what they are looking at. It might be an old musical instrument, a tool, a piece of furniture, or a hand-made something or another. Do you know what this is?

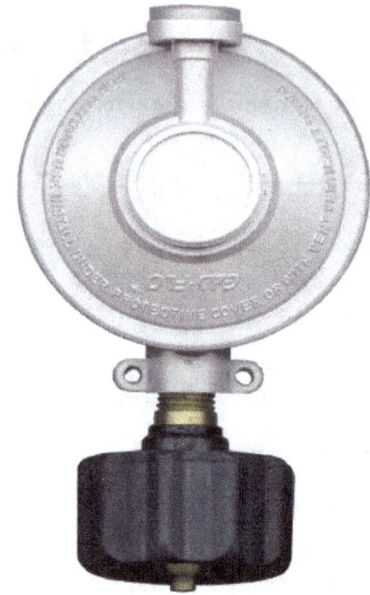

If you have ever gone camping or used a propane grill, you probably recognize the above image as a propane regulator. When functioning correctly, the propane line comes in from the top, then something *magical* happens inside the regulator, and then it comes out the bottom and passes on to your grill, appliance, etc. Then you light it with a match or lighter and just like the cavemen, you've discovered fire!

But what happens if the regulator isn't working correctly? In the best-case scenario, it shuts off the gas and you have to buy a new regulator. In the worst-case scenario, it lets too much gas through the line and when you go to light the grill… BOOOM!!

This exercise is about how best to install a regulator on your emotions. Everyone needs a regulator to adjust our emotions when we are overwhelmed. However, a regulator is not a magical black box where things happen outside of our awareness and control. Your emotional regulator is a place where you can try new things and see how they alter your feelings, thoughts, and behaviors.

There are a number of Quick Tips that you can install in your regulator to use when you need them. This way, when raw emotions enter the regulator, you will have some techniques to adjust their intensity and hopefully the outcome as well. These techniques also add deposits to your Emotional Bank Acccount!

Quick Relaxation Techniques

1. Deep breathing is a tried-and-true skill to quickly gain control of your emotions. Inhale as much as you can, then hold all that air inside you for a few seconds and then exhale while relaxing. A big inhalation expands the lungs, requiring a big exhalation to return the lungs to their resting state.

2. Try your deep breathing technique while relaxing your tongue away from the roof of your mouth and softening the muscles in your jaw.

just Breathe

3. Take a few deep breaths while running warm water over your hands.

4. Touch and tap your lips while deep breathing.

5. Sit in a chair and alternate tapping on your knees… tap your left knee with your left hand, then your right knee with your right hand. Keep a consistent rhythm going by counting or singing a song and tapping to the beat.

6. Create a playlist of music that instantly puts you in a good mood. It doesn't have to be great music but be sure it is fun music. Our favorites include "Walking on Sunshine" by Katrina, "Sweet Caroline" by Neil Diamond, "Over the Rainbow" by Israel Kamakawiwo'ole, and "Baby" by Justin Bieber. What are some of your favorites?

Imagery

Like relaxation, you can use imagery to create powerful anchors to calm your brain and manage your anxiety. Evoking imagery within your mind activates the right hemisphere of the brain and quiets your internal verbal chatter.

People often use the image of a mountain that is steady and ever-present no matter how bad the weather around the mountain becomes. Others have used the imagery of an anchor tied to their spine to "anchor" themselves into the earth when they feel depressed, upset, anxious, stressed, or angry. Imagery works particularly well if you can identify a personal image that works for you.

Coloring a Mandala

 Coloring is not just for children! Research has shown that coloring the repeating patterns and symmetrical forms of the mandala (the Sanskrit word for circle) brings a sense of calm to the mind. There are mandalas at the end of this exercise that you can use to try this activity.

Reflect & Respond

1. What techniques have you used in the past that have worked for you when regulating your emotions? Which of the techniques that we mentioned above are you willing to try?

_____

_____

_____

_____

_____

_____

2. Everyone has good intentions of trying techniques to manage their emotions however many people never follow through with their good intentions. Predict what might get in the way of your good intentions to try some of the techniques listed above.

_____

_____

_____

3. Can you think of a metaphor with very specific imagery that you can try to use to regulate your emotions?

_____

_____

_____

4. When you think of your viewing of child sexual abuse media, do you think an emotional regulator would have helped you? Why or why not?

_____

_____

_____

React

Even if you don't want to try the suggestions on this page, try them anyway. Sometimes we don't know what will work until we try it. Pick the ones that you think will work best for you. Think of some other activities that might help regulate your emotions. Talk to your friends, family, or therapist and ask how they regulate their emotions. What tools do they have in their emotional regulator?

List the three activities that you are willing to try for the next two weeks. Also list ways you are going to stay accountable to yourself to accomplish this goal.

August Flower Garden

More coloring pages at
mondaymandala.com

Badge of Honor
More coloring pages at
mondaymandala.com

Beading

More coloring pages at
mondaymandala.com

Mindfulness

One of the best "gadgets" to attach to your emotional regulators is mindfulness. Mindfulness is a popular term these days, and significant research supports the fact that it is an effective way to help people manage their emotions.

What is Mindfulness?

Mindfulness is all about existing in the present moment—paying attention to and maintaining an awareness of both your inner thoughts and the outer world around you—while accepting, rather than judging or avoiding, whatever you notice.

Mindfulness is the practice of paying attention in the moment without judgment. It can be practiced during formal meditation or used in everyday activities like cooking, cleaning, or walking.

Mindfulness is not about worrying about the future or regretting the past—it is all about the **PRESENT MOMENT!**

One of our favorite books, *Just One Thing* by Rick Hanson, Ph.D., says this about mindfulness:

"Mindfulness has a lot of benefits. It provides important information about what is happening in and around you. It helps you witness your experience without being swept away by it, and to hold it in a larger context. As your mindful awareness increases, negative experiences will have less impact on you."

Research indicates that mindfulness enhances attentional skills, self-awareness, and empathy for the emotions of others. Additionally, mindfulness helps manage and decrease negative emotions.

Practicing Mindfulness

Mindfulness is like becoming a parent to your mind rather than letting your "emotional mind" control you. By practicing mindfulness, you can teach your mind to be still and present rather than automatically reacting with emotional responses. Mindfulness helps you call on your "wise mind" to respond to situations thoughtfully.

As an extra bonus, mindfulness also disrupts the trance-like state induced by technology. Remember when you started checking your email or social media "one last time" before bed, only to realize three hours had passed? The same effect can occur when viewing pornography online—hours pass, images increase in intensity, and the ages of individuals in the images and videos get younger, etc. Rarely does anyone practice mindfulness while using technology.

Not only is mindfulness one of the most effective tools for managing emotions and creating awareness of technology use, but it is also one of the simplest. However, it takes **practice, practice, and more practice** to master the art of mindfulness. Notice we said **"simple,"** not **"easy."**

Developing a Mindfulness Practice

1. Take a walk however do not focus on your to-do list or anything that happened earlier in the day. Instead, focus on how it feels to be outside, the sensation of the air on your face, and how your body feels as it moves. Take deep breaths. Every time your mind starts to wander to the future or the past, bring your awareness back to the present moment and observe what is happening to you in a nonjudgmental way.

2. Sit quietly for two minutes. As you breathe, notice the rhythm of your

breath as you inhale and exhale. When your mind attempts to wander, gently bring your awareness back to your breathing, focusing on each inhale and exhale.

3. When having a conversation with someone, pay close attention to their words and your internal emotional responses. Remember, mindfulness is about noticing and observing!

Reflect & Respond

1. In your own words, describe your understanding of the concept of mindfulness.

_____

_____

_____

2. People who view child sexual abuse media often describe being in a "trance-like" state of mind. Thinking back to your viewing of that child sexual abuse media, do you recall the state of mind you were in? Were you in a mindful place when you were engaged in viewing child sexual abuse media.

_____

_____

_____

3. Can you describe how you think mindfulness might assist you in your efforts not to use child sexual abuse media?

_____

_____

_____

React

You can connect mindfulness to everyday life activities. What activities do you do each day that you can incorporate mindfulness into (e.g., walking, cooking, conversation with others, listening to music, etc.)? What activity can you incorporate mindfulness into during the next week? Jot down some thoughts about your mindfulness experiences.

_____

_____

_____

_____

_____

_____

_____

_____

Links to these books that can help you develop a mindfulness practice can be found on the workbook's companion website, www.internetbehavior.com/illegalimages

- *Sitting Still Like a Frog* by Eline Snel (a children's book but also a great book for adults)
- *The Buddha's Brain*, by Rick Hanson, PhD
- *Just One Thing*, by Rick Hanson, PhD
- *Palouse Mindfulness*...www.palousemindfulness.com (free!)

Chapter 3: Intimacy Skills

Intimacy is hard. It is difficult to let others get close when you aren't even sure you want to be close to yourself. Yet, you are a social being and need to find ways to connect to your community.

Technology can make intimacy even more difficult. It isn't that technology is inherently bad, but it can be used to draw you away from others and lead to isolation.

Research suggests that technology use commonly leads to increased loneliness and depression. Research also notes that technology use interferes with the ability to have empathy towards others - one of the basic building blocks of intimacy.

Do you know what else leads to loneliness, depression, and a lack of empathy? Pornography. When technology use and pornography use are combined, it creates a heavy dose of pseudo-intimacy.

This happens so frequently that psychologists even made up a word for it… "parasocial relationships." While it sounds fancy, it simply means that you feel a sense of connection with the people online that doesn't really exist. It's pretend and yet it feels real. Some men say they feel this parasocial relationship with the children in the child sexual abuse media. If that is you, remember, that is not real intimacy. It is intimacy that resides in your fantasy.

This chapter of the book is designed to help you reconnect with yourself and others. It has exercises designed to evaluate your ability to connect intimately with others. The chapter also provides ideas on how to repair identified deficits so you can experience real intimacy instead of the pseudo-intimacy offered through technology and pornography.

A List of Chapter Exercises

1. Into-Me-See
2. Do You Hear What I Hear
3. Getting to Know Renfield
4. What's Love Got to Do with It?
5. Relationships Unplugged
6. Relationship Circles
7. Won't You Be My Neighbor?

Don't Forget!

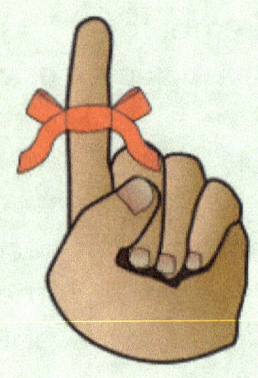

Those who have access to the Internet may want to visit our companion website for resources related to this and other chapters in the workbook. These resources include additional articles, websites, and copies of activities/graphics from the chapters.

http://www.internetbehavior.com/illegalimages.

Notes

_____

_____

_____

_____

_____

Into-Me-See

Intimacy is a concept that is often difficult to define. Our simplest definition states that intimacy occurs when you allow others to see inside of you, while they simultaneously allow you to see inside of them. Hence, "into-me-see" (sounds like intimacy if you say it fast). We know it sounds corny, but you won't forget it.

Many think that intimacy = romance = sex, but it actually has a much broader definition. Dennis Dailey, PhD, writes that intimacy is the ability to be emotionally close to another human being, and to accept their closeness in return. Individuals who view child sexual abuse media often struggle with intimacy, so addressing how you can increase intimacy in your life is a critical step towards addressing your struggle with child sexual abuse media.

Dailey suggests that intimacy is composed of several main elements:

Caring. Caring about others means we feel both their joy and their pain. We open ourselves up to their emotions in ways that may not always be comfortable or convenient, and we stay present for them emotionally as they work through their issues. Caring also suggests that we allow others to care for us. Sometimes when we go through difficult experiences, we think we have to do it on our own. But when we think that way, we deny others and ourselves intimacy.

Sharing. To have true intimacy with others, we must open up and share our inner thoughts and feelings. Although others may not always agree with our beliefs or feelings, we owe them honesty so they can make informed decisions about the relationship between us. It's risky because they may leave, but welcome to intimacy, baby! How can we truly be intimate with others if we must walk on eggshells about our true selves? Also, when you create relationships with others, do you make them feel welcome and safe to share their true selves with you? If you don't, you may be putting out vibes to others that they should not share important things with you.

Vulnerability. Intimacy requires risk-taking behaviors that make us vulnerable. After all, those we seek intimacy with may reject us, abandon us, judge us, gossip about us, etc. When we seek out intimacy, we inevitably open ourselves up to the possibility of negative things. But, unless we make ourselves vulnerable, we will never truly allow people to get close to us. As Brené Brown, a famous pop-culture figure and author, states, "Courage starts with showing up and letting ourselves be seen." This works both ways – can you be vulnerable AND tolerate it when others are allowing you to see their vulnerability? (see "Caring" above)

Here are ten suggested skills that address the three elements of intimacy mentioned above:

1. Spending time and being present with friends/family/partners.

2. Making eye contact while you are communicating.

3. Disclosing something personal about yourself.

4. Saying what you are thinking in compassionate, caring ways.

5. Practicing rigorous honesty (not brutal, cruel honesty).

6. Practicing mindful listening skills (see "Do You Hear" exercise).

7. Asking for and accepting feedback from others.

8. Staying present when conversations get difficult.

9. Discussing intimacy in your relationships.

10. Allowing others to care for you when you need help.

Reflect & Respond

1. The University of Intimacy has announced a new patent on a machine that allows you and others to "see" your level of intimacy skills. It's called the "Intimacy X-Ray Machine." This machine has the ability to remove your skin, bones, organs, and blood to look directly into your body and view your true ability to be emotionally intimate with others. Write some words on the X-Ray illustration below that represent your intimacy skills. Use large, green letters for writing those skills you feel have developed well. In medium-sized, orange letters, write the skills you are making progress with. And in small, red letters, write the skills you hope to develop.

Intimacy X-Ray

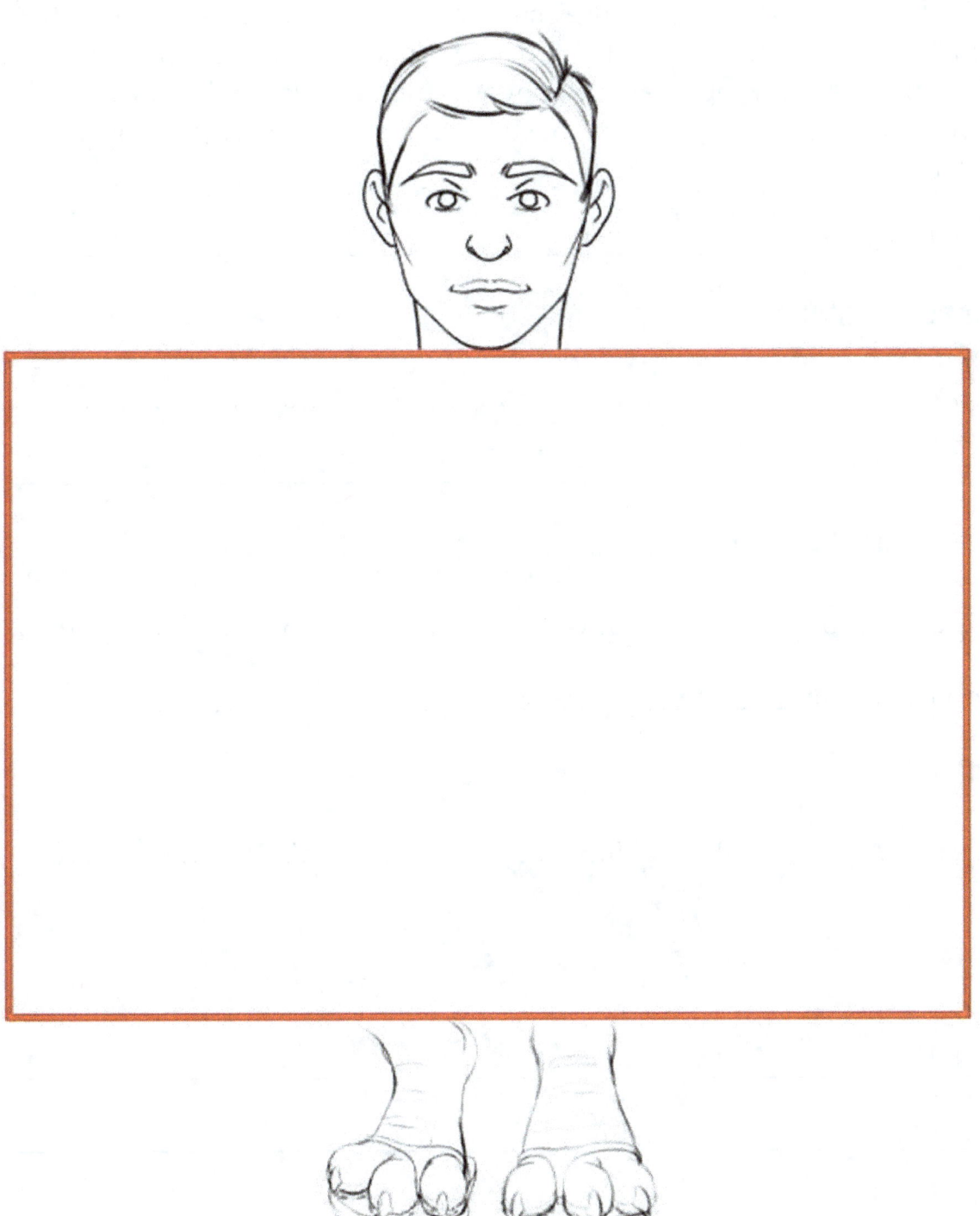

React #1

In the space below, provide the names of several close people in your life. They may be friends or partners, but they should all be people that you have (or would like to have) intimacy with. Below their name is a scale from 1 to 10. Circle the number that best represents the level of intimacy you believe you have with that person. Think about what you have read and try to be rigorously honest about it.

Person #1 Name: _____

Intimacy Scale:

1........2.........3.........4.........5.........6.........7.........8.........9.........10

Person #2 Name: _____

Intimacy Scale:

1........2.........3.........4.........5.........6.........7.........8.........9.........10

Person #3 Name: _____

Intimacy Scale:

1........2.........3.........4.........5.........6.........7.........8.........9.........10

Notes

_____

_____

_____

_____

React #2

Now go back and review each of your ratings. Imagine what it would take to move the rating up one number. For example, if you rated your relationship with someone as a six (6), what intimacy skill (caring, sharing, vulnerability) would it take to move it to a seven (7)? Make a concrete plan about how you will attempt to increase intimacy with each of these people.

Person #1 Intimacy Plan

_____

_____

_____

Person #2 Intimacy Plan

_____

_____

_____

Person #3 Intimacy Plan

_____

_____

_____

Notes

_____

_____

Do You Hear What I Hear

Listening is an important skill in any relationship. Think back to the Seven Desires from Chapter 1. Listening always helps people feel heard and understood, affirmed, included, chosen, safe, blessed, and emotionally touched. Listening can strengthen every relationship in each of those four circles.

Listening really is the "miracle" skill that improves almost any relationship. While it seems as though listening to what the people in our lives are saying should be easy, it turns out that **being present** and truly **LISTENING** is a very difficult skill to master. Review the Six Keys to Effective Listening.

1. Quiet your mind and focus on the other person.

2. Face the person squarely and make eye contact.

3. Listen fully and openly to what they are saying.

4. Listen "through" the words to the deeper meaning and underlying needs (Seven Desires) that you sense from the person.

5. Don't interrupt the person as they are speaking.

6. When they are finished speaking, in your own words, repeat back to the person what they said and the feelings that you sensed from them, so they know you are really **LISTENING**.

Inside our heads, most of us are thinking about something in the past or the future while supposedly listening to others. We often develop our response to what we think the other person will say before they have even finished speaking. Rarely do we take the time to wonder with real curiosity about the deeper needs of the person we are speaking with. How often do we interrupt the person speaking because we are too bored or too anxious to keep our thoughts to ourselves?

Really listening to others requires all the mindfulness skills you learned about in the previous chapter on emotional management. Mindfulness skills are particularly helpful when working to become a better listener.

Create a "Listening Ear" using the picture on the next page. Draw pictures, create symbols, paste pictures, and/or write words representing the Six Keys to Effective Listening.

Reflect & Respond

1. Which one of the Six Keys to Effective Listening is your biggest strength?

    _____

    _____

    _____

2. Which one of the Six Keys to Effective Listening is your biggest weakness?

    _____

    _____

    _____

    _____

    _____

    _____

React

Share your "Listening Ear" with your partner, friend, family member, therapist, and/or therapy group. Ask for feedback on how well you do with each of the Six Keys to Effective Listening. Be sure to use those Six Keys to Effective Listening to HEAR the feedback you are receiving.

Make an effort to use the Six Keys to Effective Listening for the next two weeks. Journal about your experience and/or share your experience with the people in your support network or with your therapist or your therapy group.

Notes

_____

_____

_____

_____

Getting to Know Renfield

Do you know the story of Renfield? He was Dracula's sidekick, but he was also a victim of Dracula. Banished to a cell (victim role), he had to work hard each day to survive while endlessly serving Dracula (survivor role), always hoping to earn Dracula's love and approval if he just worked hard enough (servant role). Renfield would endure his situation until he couldn't take it any longer, at which point he would "flip," transforming into a vampire (perpetrator role). As a vampire, he would destroy others to fulfill his own needs, but when morning arrived, he would revert to his roles of victim, survivor, and servant to Dracula.

The image below perfectly illustrates Renfield's dual nature. On the right side of the wall is his victim, survivor, and servant side. He looks weak and downtrodden, with a muzzle over his mouth to silence his own needs and truth. His middle finger is chewed off, preventing him from even gesturing his defiance to the world. Yet, despite everything, he survives to fight another day.

The vampire side of Renfield is on the left side of the wall. This is who he becomes when he can't stand it any longer and "flips." As a vampire, he finally satisfies his thirst for blood, regardless of whom he harms or the consequences he may face.

The Vampire | **The Perfect Servant**

We often see this dynamic and its four related roles—(a) victim, (b) survivor, (c) servant, and (d) perpetrator—manifest in individuals who struggle with intimacy. Such individuals often take on one or more of these roles in their relationships, which ultimately hinders their ability to form meaningful connections. When people don't have their intimacy needs met in healthy ways, things can get ugly.

The Four Roles of Renfield

Victim ("It's not my fault.")

Those in the victim role often act out of deep emotional pain. They feel defeated and, for the most part, have given up. They expect poor treatment and don't believe they deserve much from others in relationships. Some people resist identifying as a victim because it makes them feel weak or needy. When faced with consequences, individuals in this role may make excuses or rationalize their negative behaviors, offering justifications for the harm they've caused.

Survivor ("I work so hard.")

A person in the survivor role has endured significant hardships—such as a difficult upbringing, failed relationships, academic struggles, substance abuse, or time in treatment—and emerged with their humanity intact. This role conveys toughness, dedication, and resilience. Survivors don't expect much improvement in their circumstances, but they never give up.

Servant ("I give so much.")

The servant prioritizes pleasing others, often at the expense of their own well-being. They take responsibility for others' happiness and are even willing to accept blame if it makes someone else feel better. Those in this role believe that if they just do a little more or do things a little better, they will finally earn love and respect.

Perpetrator ("I deserve it all.")

This role is often hidden, buried under layers of suppressed anger and resentment from years of feeling like a victim, survivor, or servant. The perpetrator believes they are entitled to whatever they desire because they have suffered, worked hard, and sacrificed for others. They justify getting their needs met at the expense of others.

Remember Hermes' Web from Chapter 1 of this workbook? The perpetrator emerges when the "flip" occurs. After all, a person can only suppress the victim, survivor, and servant roles for so long before the pressure builds and forces a dramatic shift.

Reflect & Respond

1. Do you recognize yourself in the Renfield roles? Describe how you take on the roles of victim, survivor, servant, and/or vampire (perpetrator). Which of the roles is your most prominent role(s)?

_____

_____

_____

2. Where did this role originate for you? Were there things in your childhood that encouraged the development of this role for you?

_____

_____

_____

_____

_____

3. How do you believe your prominent role(s) interferes with getting your intimacy needs met?

_____

_____

_____

4. How do you think your prominent role(s) influenced your decision to use of child sexual abuse media? How did your role influence you inability to find deeper intimacy in your relationships?

_____

_____

_____

Notes

_____

_____

_____

_____

_____

_____

_____

_____

React

Now that you understand each of Renfield's roles, complete the table below.

In the far-left column, list the characteristics of "Renfield" that you identify with the most. Do you feel like a victim? Do you feel that no one cares about you? Do you get tired of caring for others? Do you feel like you are just trying to survive in life? Do you turn into an angry, abusive individual at times?

In the middle column, see if you can recognize the areas of your life when Renfield's roles show up the most. Do you struggle with friends and family? In romantic relationships? At work? At school?

Finally, use the right column to list healthy ways to avoid falling into the negative roles associated with Renfield. Examples might include taking responsibility and ownership for your own feelings, decisions, and behaviors, not overextending yourself when you have no resources to give, learning to share more about yourself, sharing your feelings of frustration in the moment and not letting them build up, etc.

Learning to recognize the roles you easily fall into with others and learning healthier ways to avoid these negative roles will assist you in becoming better equipped at getting your intimacy needs met.

**To purchase the toy set with the Vampire and the Perfect Servant, visit www.hermesweb.com.

Notes

_____

_____

_____

_____

Which of the Renfield Roles (victim, survivor, servant, perpetrator) Do You Identify with Most?	Where, When, Why, and with Whom Do the Renfield roles show up?	Healthy Ways to Avoid the Renfield Roles

What's Love Got to Do with It?

A famous psychologist named Robert Sternberg once developed a theory of love, which he called the *Triangular Theory of Love*. Sternberg believed that all relationships could be defined by three main components of love: (1) commitment, (2) intimacy, and (3) passion. And because he was so brilliant, he thought, "Since there are three components, why not use them to make a triangle?" Not really that brilliant but a great idea! He then described the seven types of loving relationships that result from combining these three components.

Now, you may be asking, "What's Love Got to Do with It?" Well, by understanding the various types of relationships formed by Sternberg's triangle, our hope is that you will gain insight into why you turned to using child sexual abuse media to get your "love needs" met.

Below are Sternberg's seven triangles. Note that when a side of the triangle is 'illuminated,' that indicates the presence of that love component in the relationship.

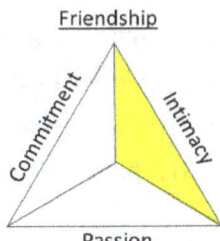

When the intimacy side of the triangle is the only one that is illuminated, it indicates that you have a friendship with someone. In these relationships, you simply enjoy the emotional closeness and intimacy of "hanging out" and spending time together. You can go out to eat, enjoy a movie together, and learn interpersonally from one another.

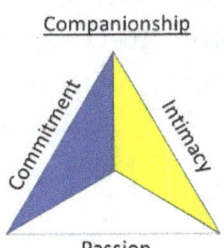

Add commitment to the relationship and suddenly the triangle moves from a friendship into a more valuable form of companionship. Not only do you enjoy the occasional emotional closeness, but you are committed to putting effort into the relationship and making sure it will last long-term. You are willing to sacrifice things for this person and to foster a mutual commitment with intimacy.

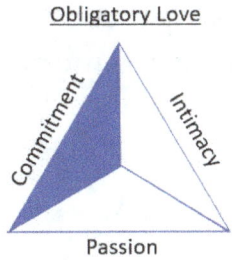

What happens when you have commitment without intimacy? The result of this triangle is the experience of obligatory love. This is love that is present because of an obligation. We often see this when a child has a strained relationship with their parents as they age. While they don't experience intimacy in the relationship, they still feel obligated to take care of their aging parents. This may also be present in "have to" friendships or abusive relationships.

Passion is the physical and sexual contact in some relationships. When passion is the ONLY side of the triangle illuminated, it just creates an infatuation for the other person.

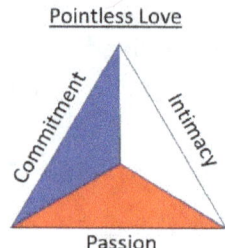

Some people may call this a "f*** buddy." It may also be the motivation for your use of child sexual abuse media, either because of an interest in anything sexual in the online environment or because of a specific sexual interest in children. This triangle has no commitment or intimacy; it is simply about sexually objectifying others with no feelings or obligation.

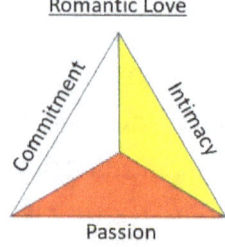

What happens when you add commitment to the passion? It creates pointless love. In the absence of intimacy, this triangle represents a relationship where there is no long-term point to love. Sternberg would say these relationships are "pointless" because, while they can exist and even feel good in the short term, the road ahead is always a dead end.

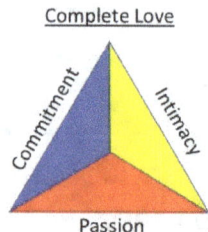

So, what does the combination of intimacy and passion create? Romantic love. Which sounds nice, right? However, it is important to keep in mind that the lack of commitment to the other person calls into question how long this honeymoon phase of passion can last. Relationships usually begin with this triangle, but how many times have we heard, "He just won't commit." This translates to, "I don't see a future here."

Finally, when all three segments of the triangle are illuminated, Sternberg says that love is complete - at least in a committed sexual relationship. This would be his goal for partnered couples with romantic interests.

Many people who use child sexual abuse media illuminate the "intimacy" and/or "passion/sex" aspect of the triangle, leading them to believe that they can get their intimacy and/or sexual needs by using sex online, including child sexual abuse media.

Reflect & Respond

1. Think about three current relationships you have in your life. Color in the sections of the triangles below that represent those relationships. Write the name of the person to the left of the triangle. Match the triangle to the above triangles and place the name of that type of love on the line above the triangle.

Person	Fill in the Triangle
	_____ Love Commitment Intimacy Passion
	_____ Love Commitment Intimacy Passion
	_____ Love Commitment Intimacy Passion

2. As you examine the types of love in your life (starting with the three you listed above), do you notice any aspects that are missing in your life? If so, list these missing elements below.

_____

_____

_____

3. What role, if any, do you believe the missing part of love may have played in your use of child sexual abuse media?

_____

_____

_____

_____

_____

React

On the triangle below, write at least three ideas in each section of the triangle about how you would develop that particular area in a healthy way. For example, if you hope to develop more intimacy with a family member, you may initiate a meeting with them (getting coffee, going on a hike or a road trip, etc.) with the goal of talking more personally and intimately with them. After completing this exercise, choose at least one idea from the triangle and try to implement it with someone. Get accountability by sharing your plan with a friend, therapist, or group.

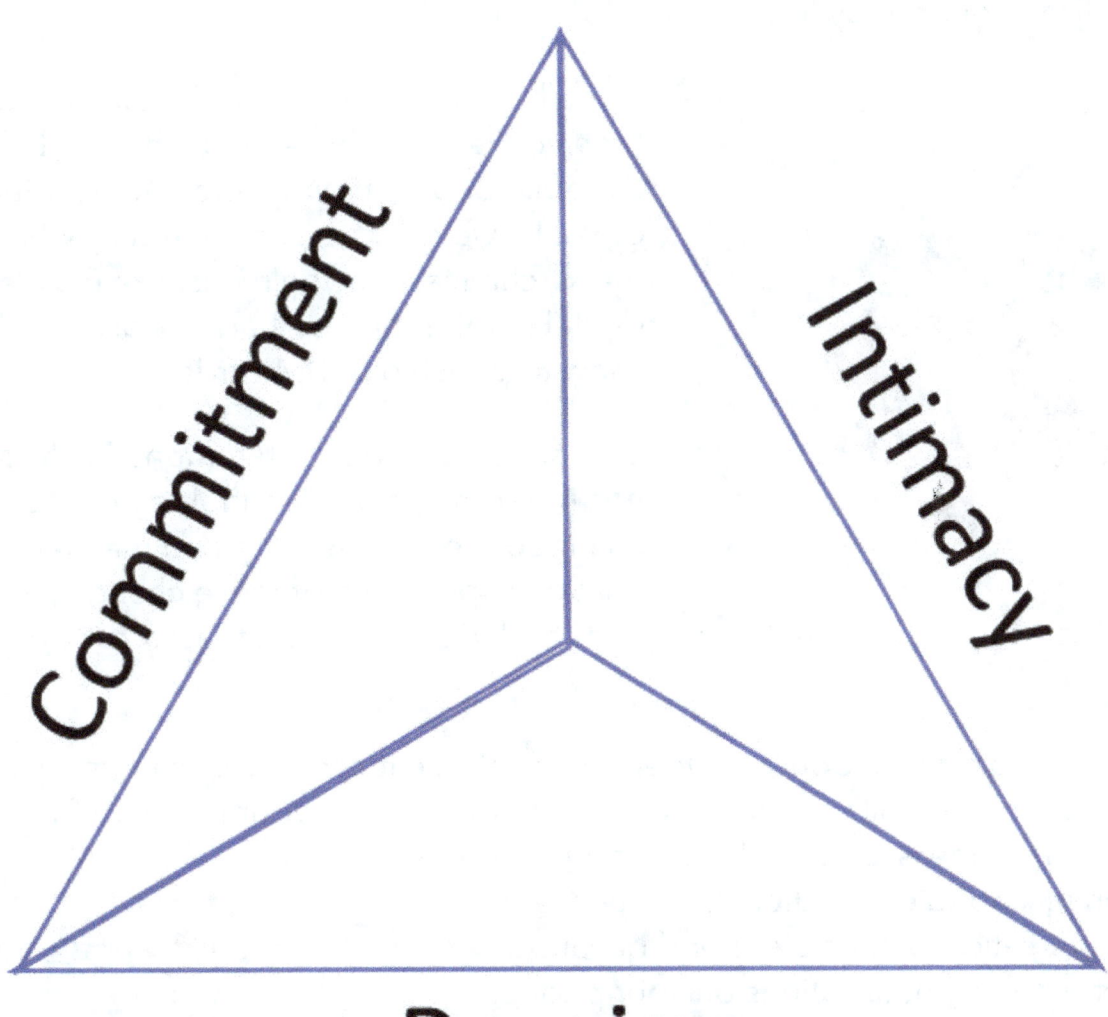

Relationships Unplugged

Connect that 300-baud modem to the landline and dial-up AOL. It's busy. Redial. Once connected, go to the keyboard of your TRS-80 computer and fire up AIM to see who's logged in from your buddy list.

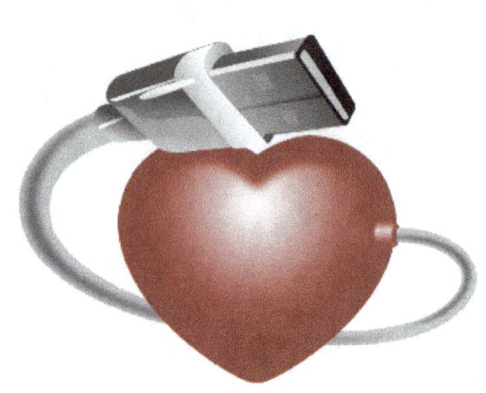

If you have no idea what we're talking about, then you're probably a digital native—born with a mobile phone in one hand and a tablet in the other. However, if you know exactly what we mean, chances are you're just like us. We are digital immigrants—we had to walk uphill in the snow to punch our IBM cards.

Let's start with a basic statement: **Technology is not inherently bad.** Technology has certainly changed the way we form and maintain relationships. Some of these changes are great! Today, we can stay in touch with loved ones and friends in ways that were impossible 30 years ago.

However, technology is a double-edged sword. While it can increase intimacy and closeness, it can also pull us apart. You're out to dinner with your family or friends, and you realize everyone is looking down at their phones rather than talking to each other. You struggle to have a conversation with an old friend because you're distracted by notifications on your phone. What are some examples of how technology has interfered with your relationships?

How have you allowed technology to pull you out of relationships with others? Maybe you're the one who ignores family members just to scroll mindlessly on your phone. Perhaps you sneak a look at your email under the table while out to eat. Remember that invitation you turned down to socialize with others because you preferred a night at home with your technology (or pornography)? Can you even recall the last **heart-to-heart** conversation you had with someone while looking them in the eye?

You might be wondering what this has to do with viewing child sexual abuse media.

The answer is that many people start by viewing adult pornography and then eventually turn to child sexual abuse media to alleviate loneliness and create a sense of pseudo-intimacy. People often fall into the trap of using sex online because it's a quick and easy way to feel connected without the "hassles" of building real relationships in the offline world.

Remember, there are many ways to experience pleasure.

Technology provides multiple opportunities to flood your brain with dopamine without ever touching your genitals. Have you ever thought of your technology use as a form of self-gratification? Scrolling? Text messaging? Likes and follows? What else? These could all be considered forms of self-stimulation, as they provide a dopamine "hit," much like physical gratification.

When there is a lack of true intimacy in your life, you may be more drawn to online sex, which can eventually lead to viewing child sexual abuse media or engaging in harmful discussions about the sexual abuse of children.

The goal is to recognize that while the online world helps us stay connected to important people in our lives, it can also give us a false sense of intimacy through online-only relationships (sometimes called pseudo-intimacy or parasocial relationships). To maintain emotional and relational health, we must cultivate strong, meaningful offline relationships that balance our connection to technology.

Reflect & Respond

1. Do you think you used the online environment to find a sense of connection and intimacy with other people? To you find a sense of connection and intimacy with your legal and/or illegal pornography use.

_____

_____

_____

2. Do you struggle with intimacy in the offline environment? If so, what are some of the problems you experience with intimacy?

_____

_____

_____

3. Consider what others say about your intimacy skills. Does your self-assessment of your intimacy skills match what others say about your intimacy skills?

_____

_____

_____

4. Consider ways to increase your comfortableness with intimacy with others (e.g., practice socializing with others, share a secret with someone, invite someone to breakfast, etc.) Make a list of things you could do to increase your intimacy with others.

_____

_____

_____

React

On the picture of the computer monitor on the next page, brainstorm the pros and cons of how technology affects your intimate relationships with others. Think about your family? Acquaintances? Friendships? Romantic partners?

Show your list of pros and cons to a couple of people you know (friends, family, group members, etc.) to see if they can help add more to your list.

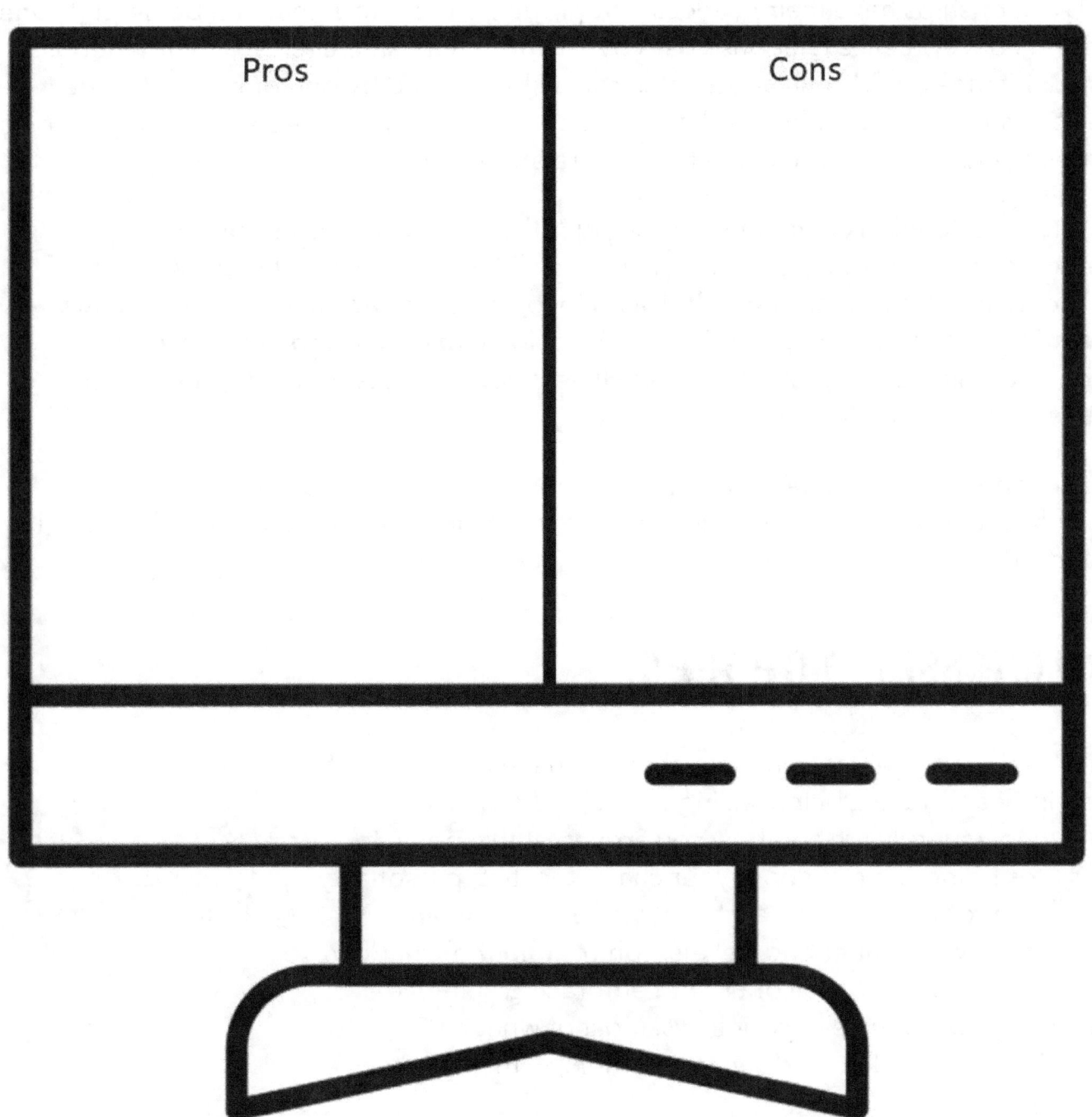

Pros

Cons

Relationship Circles

All relationships have their nuances, but grouping them together can be helpful. One way to conceptualize relationships is by using "relationship circles." Family, friends, acquaintances, work colleagues, etc., can all be defined by one or more of these relationship circles. Understanding these circles will help you recognize the different types of intimacy you can expect in each relationship.

While we often think of intimacy as being "other" focused, it is important to remember that intimacy begins with yourself. This is why the first circle we discuss is the **Relationship with the Self**. This is followed by **Relationships of the Heart, Relationships of the Path,** and finally, **Relationships Involving Transactions**. Understanding each of these circles will help you evaluate and comprehend the different types of relationships in your life.

Remember, no one circle is more important than another. In fact, we should strive to cultivate relationships that fall into all of these circles to achieve a well-balanced "portfolio" of people in our lives.

RELATIONSHIP WITH THE SELF

This circle represents the relationship you have with yourself. Self-intimacy means being willing to take a deep dive into who you truly are and how you arrived at this point. It involves being curious about your characteristics, personality traits, thoughts, decisions, and behaviors. It also means examining your values and beliefs, confronting the "shadow side" that exists within all of us, and embracing self-love—including acceptance of your flaws. Most of what belongs to this circle is often kept hidden from others, with only a few exceptions.

RELATIONSHIPS OF THE HEART

This circle consists of the people with whom we share deep intimacy, including our secrets and heartfelt emotions. These are the people we feel closest to, and this group may or may not include family members. People in this circle are often in our lives for the long term. Even if we move to a new city, change jobs, or graduate from school, our connection with them remains strong. A change in circumstances does not weaken the bond we share with them. It is a true relationship of the heart.

RELATIONSHIPS OF THE PATH

While you may also share significant intimacy with the people in this circle, the relationship is primarily based on the fact that your paths have intersected at some point. If circumstances were to change, the level of intimacy in this relationship would likely change as well. Co-workers and neighbors are common examples of relationships in this circle. If we move or change jobs, we often lose contact with these people, and the relationship does not endure over time.

There is nothing wrong with these types of relationships—we all need them. However, we must recognize that as our paths change, so will these relationships.

RELATIONSHIPS INVOLVING TRANSACTIONS

These people are in our circle because we share a superficial (but still real!) relationship with them. Sometimes, we refer to these relationships as "acquaintances." They may be individuals you could call if you needed a ride somewhere or wanted to borrow a tool, but there is little to no real intimacy shared.

While these relationships may not be deeply personal, they are still valuable and can provide us with certain aspects of connection and social interaction.

Reflect & Respond

1. How well do you know yourself? Do you believe you are able to honest with yourself about your strengths and your faults? Are you aware of the characteristics about yourself that tend to annoy others.

    _____

    _____

    _____

2. After taking an honest look at yourself do you feel like that overall, you like who you are and enjoying "hanging out" with yourself? How can you improve your relationship with yourself?

    _____

    _____

    _____

3. What are some of the barriers you experience to making and maintaining relationships with the individuals in your various circles? Do you have social anxiety? Have you been burned by relationships in the past and have difficulty trusting people? Are you just an introvert?

    _____

    _____

    _____

    _____

4. Which circle(s) makes you most uncomfortable? In what ways does the circle(s) make your uncomfortable?

_____

_____

_____

5. What steps do you need to take to improve your Heart, Path, and Transaction circles? How can you "balance" your relationship portfolio?

_____

_____

_____

React

In the circle illustration on the next page, list three to five people currently in your life that fit into each of the circles (heart, path, transactional). If you are having difficulty with this exercise, that is a sign that you need to broaden your horizon of friends. Intimate relationships help prevent the viewing of child sexual abuse media. A broad range of intimate relationships serve as "protective factors" in preventing problematic behaviors.

The more people you have in your circles, the more support you have on your journey. For proper mental health and wellbeing, it is suggested that you have at least five people in each circle and a solid relationship with yourself.

Relationship Circles

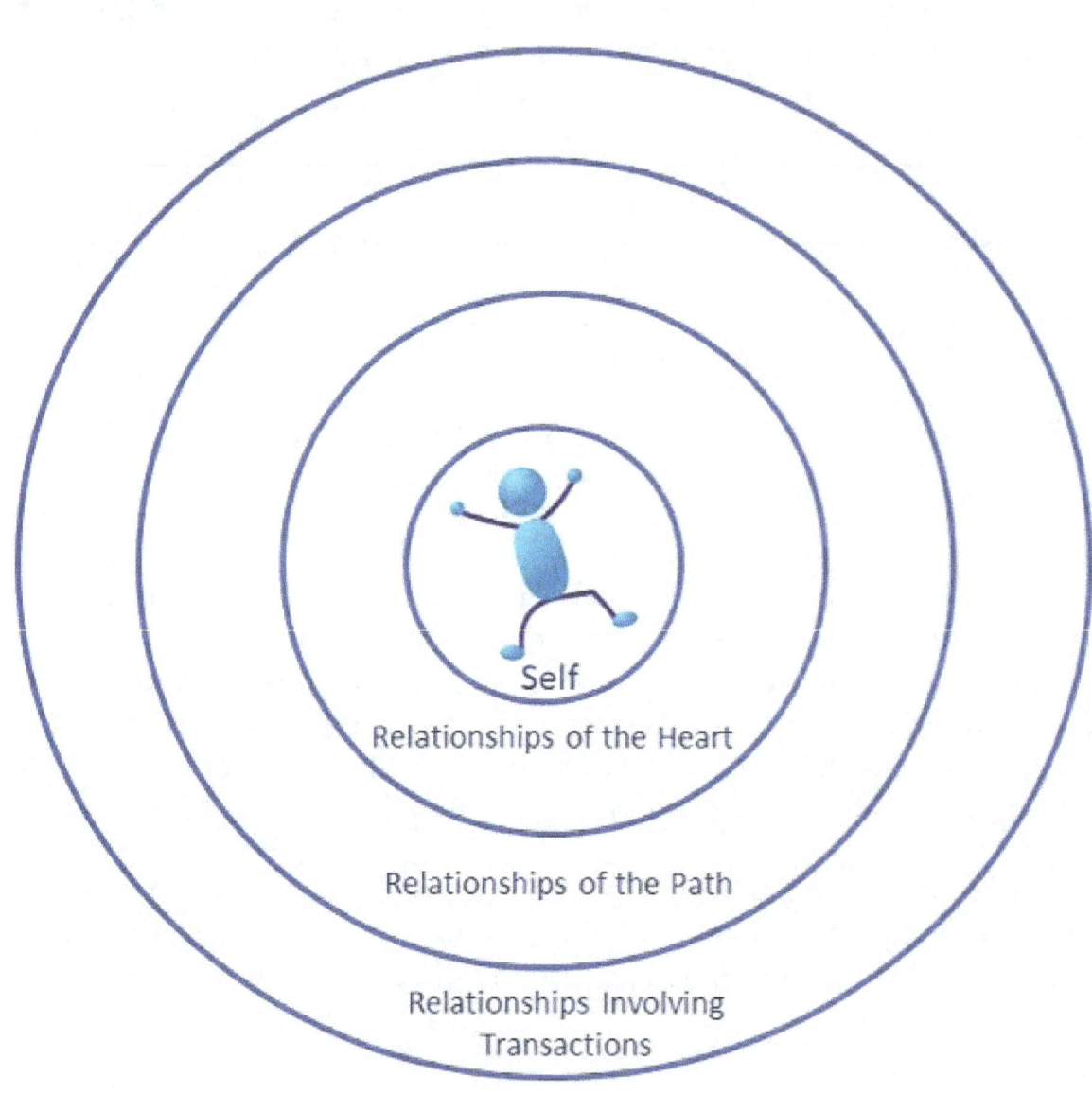

Self

Relationships of the Heart

Relationships of the Path

Relationships Involving
Transactions

Won't You Be My Neighbor?

Surrounding yourself with a supportive and encouraging community is central to engaging in healthy relationships. Without a positive community around you, it is nearly impossible to successfully move away from child sexual abuse media.

This chapter of the workbook has already discussed many ideas and skills to help you develop and maintain healthy relationships with other individuals, but it is also important to think about how to begin fostering your relationships with groups and organizations as you build your larger community.

So, What Is "Community"?

A community is a group of individuals or organizations who share a common set of goals, goals which include assisting the members of that community. One way to think about how a community can come together to achieve its goals is to revisit the Seven Desires we discussed earlier in Chapter 1. While no community helps you meet all of your Seven Desires, communities often provide some of the Seven Desires by:

- Fostering the feeling that you are heard and understood by others.
- Affirming that you are a valuable member of the community.

- Expecting nothing from you and accepting you into the community.
- Assuring your safety in all areas - physical, emotional, sexual, etc.
- Providing physical intimacy, including shaking hands, hugs, etc.
- Choosing you specifically, indicating that you are worthy.
- Including you, regardless of your shortcomings and misdeeds.

Below are some examples of organizations, institutions, and resources that can help you in creating a community. It is unlikely that you will have access to all of these, and quite possible that you may think of others you can add as well. This list is to just get you started thinking about the larger context of community.

Some community building resources include:

- Community Centers
- Places of Worship
- Educational Institutions
  - Community Colleges / Universities
- Medical Services
  - Psychiatry / Medications
  - Hospitals
- Workplaces
- Friends and Family
- Social Services / Mental Health
  - Therapists, 12-Step Groups, Therapy Groups, etc.
- Parks and Recreations Areas
  - Hobbies and Leisure Activities

Can you think of others?

It is important to remember that not everyone in your community needs to know about your struggle with child sexual abuse media. However, some members of your community will need to know about that struggle so they can provide you with specific types of support. These community members may include close friends, family members, or a therapist. It's difficult to know who to tell and who not to tell. We suggest you discuss this issue with a therapist or your probation officer so they can help you make the correct decision.

Reflect & Respond

1. Look at the list of community examples above and think about YOUR community of support. List below those organizations and institutions that create community for you.

    _____

    _____

    _____

2. Revisit the list of the Seven Desires and how your community can help you meet these desires by:

    *   Fostering the feeling that you are heard and understood by others.
    *   Affirming that you are a valuable member of the community.
    *   Expecting nothing from you and accepting you into the community.
    *   Assuring your safety in all areas - physical, emotional, sexual, etc.
    *   Providing physical intimacy, including shaking hands, hugs, etc.
    *   Choosing you specifically, indicating that you are worthy.
    *   Including you, regardless of your shortcomings and misdeeds.

    Based on this list and those organizations and institutions you listed in question #1, can you see how your community is helping you meet your Seven Desires?

    _____

    _____

    _____

    _____

3. List the people in your community who know about your use of child sexual abuse media. Do you think this is enough people to provide you with the necessary support? Have you considered telling other individuals or groups? If so, who would that be?

_____

_____

_____

_____

_____

_____

_____

React

Sometimes, it helps to map out your community so you can see all the resources you have to support you on your journey. Use the neighborhood map below to draw/write the names of your community's people, institutions, and organizations. Circle those pictures/words that provide you with the most support and place a star next to those you want to strengthen. Are there any institutions that are not on your community map which you would like to add? If so, list them on the bottom of your map page.

Suppose you can't think of anyone to list as a part of your community. In that case, it is important to take the first step in creating that community as soon as possible. Return to the list of possible community building resources and determine what person, institution, or organization you will add in the next week. If you are uncertain who to add first, we would suggest starting with a therapist who can support you in adding others to your community.

Chapter 4: Deviant Sexuality

Deviant? Why use such an offensive word to describe sexuality? Well, the fact is sometimes we give words too much meaning. The word "deviant" simply means "different from what most people do." It means to "deviate" from the norm. And as we all know, normalcy is a broadly debated concept! However, in the world of sexuality (even among groups that accept many forms of sexual behavior) when an individual has sexual interest in, or arousal to, children (defined as those who have not fully developed through puberty), they are considered deviant from the norm group. While we debated using the term in this workbook, it is important to note that approximately 10% of the population has some sexual curiosity, interest, or arousal related to children while 90% do not. Therefore, we decided the term "deviant sexuality" applies to the topic of using child sexual abuse media.

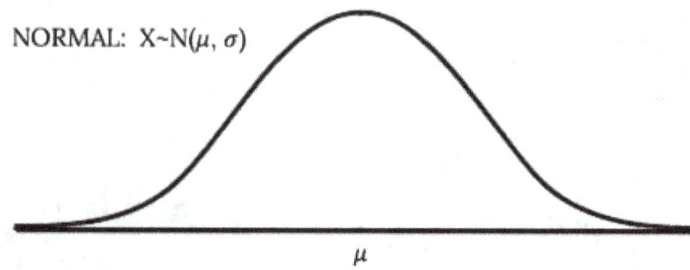

You might be saying to yourself, "Wait! I do not have sexual interest in children. I am not attracted to kids!" While we recognize there are a number of reasons why someone may view child sexual abuse media, we also need to acknowledge that there must have been some curiosity, interest, or arousal present for you to seek out this kind of media. Otherwise, you would have chosen some other negative, unhealthy habit to satisfy yourself. Drugs, perhaps? Regardless, it is important to recognize you must have derived some amount of pleasure or relief in viewing child sexual abuse media (even if it was surprising and temporary) or else you wouldn't have viewed it.

The purpose of this chapter is to get you thinking about your deviant sexuality. We want to increase your understanding and awareness as well as provide you with some exercises that may be helpful in managing this issue in your life.

There are many factors that can contribute to the development of deviant sexual interests or arousal related to children. Some professionals believe the beginnings of such deviant sexual interests are formed in the womb, before someone is even born. Others believe there is a genetic predisposition towards sexually deviant behaviors that gets triggered at some point during a person's life. Yet another belief is that deviant sexual interests is developed as a response to certain traumatic experiences.

The truth is this: we just don't know what exactly causes sexual interest in children or arousal to children. In fact, deviant sexuality likely has multiple causes, and so it might be the case that all the previous theories are true.

Many people wonder if their sexual interest in children will ever go away. For some, when they stop viewing child sexual abuse media, there interest and arousal does begin to dissipate. For others, it may be a lifelong issue that never really goes away. The majority of individuals probably fall between these two ends of the continuum.

It is important to remember that you are not sexually deviant, but your behavior is. Separating out who you are from your behaviors is the first key to freedom from your shame and despair about the use of child sexual abuse media. Clients will often say that their sexual interest/arousal in children has consumed every aspect of their life, and they feel that they don't have an identity outside of that. We are here to say that your use of child sexual abuse media is just one aspect of who you are. It does not define you. It's time to let the world see the rest of you!

A List of Chapter Exercises

1. Sexuality Soup
2. Healthy Sexuality
3. True North
4. The 13th Witch
5. The Dark Side of the Brain
6. The Big "M"
7. Two For the Price of One

Don't forget!

Those who have access to the Internet may want to visit our companion website for resources related to this and other chapters in the workbook. These resources include additional articles, websites, and copies of activities/graphics from the chapters.

http://www.internetbehavior.com/illegalimages

Notes

_____

_____

_____

_____

_____

_____

_____

_____

_____

_____

Sexuality Soup

Boys have penises. Girls have vaginas. Ok… we aren't really starting there, but we will be starting with a more advanced version of "The Birds and the Bees" talk that you may have received as a child. This advanced discussion centers around how our sexuality develops and takes shape over the course of our lifetime. It is about understanding the non-genital part of sex - the part that really matters!

Understanding that sexuality is more complex than genitalia is really important. After all, the largest sex organ in the body is… the brain! It might seem odd to begin with the advanced Birds and Bees discussion in a chapter of the workbook focused on deviant sexual behavior, but until you understand your sexual self and how you arrived here, you won't be able to fully develop healthy sexuality for yourself.

Let's begin with one of our favorite graphics – "YouSoup Recipe." Full credit for this graphic and accompanying information goes to Sam Killermann. Essentially, Sam asserts that each of us is a simmering pot of soup, and like any good soup, there is a wide variety of ingredients that come together to form our particular flavor. Once we are done cooking, the soup tastes different because different ingredients were added along the way.

Those ingredients may include your race, your gender, how much money your family had growing up, your early childhood experiences, your education, your culture, your religion, your career, your political beliefs, your interactions with others, and hidden aspects of yourself. The combination of all these different "ingredients" creates who you are as a person, both generally and sexually. Given the nature of this workbook, today we are going to have you focus on your "sexuality soup."

YOUSOUP Recipe version2 *it's pronounced* METRO♂sexual

Ingredients:

base & broth
- race
- ethnicity
- gender
- sexuality

early additions
- socioeconomic status
- geographic location
- education
- family structure

optional
- hobbies & passions
- religion & faith
- career
- political beliefs

secret ingredients
- personal experiences
- changes to other ingredients
- hidden identities
- misperception of ingredients

Procedure:

Combine base ingredients to create broth and bring to a boil. Toss in early additions and simmer over low heat for many, many years, adding optional and secret ingredients to taste. Makes one You.

Take a look at the graphic that outlines the common categories of ingredients in our sexuality soup. In the bowl of soup below, list some of the ingredients in YOUR sexuality soup recipe. You can draw them or write words in the soup. Think about all the areas in the YouSoup graphic that might apply to you and your sexuality. For example, what aspects of gender, family, and religion may have influenced your sexuality? What personal experiences, including those things that you may choose to keep hidden from others, have impacted your sexuality? Your soup will have ingredients from childhood through the present day.

Reflect & Respond

1. As you reflect on your sexuality soup ingredients, what aspects of your life influence your sexuality the most? Is it your early childhood experiences? Your experiences with family, peers, or others? Maybe your religion or your career? If you experienced abuse or trauma, how might those particular experiences have affected the flavor of your sexuality soup?

    _____

    _____

    _____

2. Not all ingredients are bad – many make our sexuality soup taste great! However, what ingredients can you identify that make your sexuality soup taste bad? That is, what do you wish was left out of the recipe? *(Personally, I hate cilantro!)* Is it possible to remove those ingredients? How might you remove them? Would you rather develop a different sexuality soup recipe altogether? If so, what would that look like?

    _____

    _____

    _____

3. What part of your sexuality soup recipe do you think contributed to your use of child sexual abuse media? If those parts of your sexuality soup were addressed, would that decrease the likelihood that you would view these illegal images again?

    _____

    _____

    _____

4. What's the plan for addressing these parts of your sexuality soup that need more understanding and/or healing? Counseling? Self-Care? What else?

_____

_____

_____

Notes

_____

_____

_____

_____

_____

_____

_____

_____

_____

_____

_____

_____

Healthy Sexuality

The focus of this chapter is on addressing deviant sexuality. But to understand unhealthy sexuality, we must first re-examine your ideas about healthy sexuality.

For some of you, this may mean returning to a time in your life when your sexual thoughts, feelings, fantasies, urges, and behaviors were healthy (or at the very least, healthier than they are now). But for others, you may feel as though your sexuality has never truly been healthy. Either way, this exercise will help you understand (and

hopefully develop) a sense of what it means to be sexually healthy. In this exercise, you will work to understand the components of sexual health and develop a plan to achieve a definition of healthy sexuality that fits you!

Let's begin by reviewing the World Health Organization's definition of sexual health:

"Sexual health is a state of physical, emotional, mental and social well-being in relation to sexuality; it is not merely the absence of disease, dysfunction, or infirmity. Sexual health requires a positive and respectful approach to sexuality and sexual relationships, as well as the possibility of having pleasurable and safe sexual experiences free of coercion, discrimination, and violence. For sexual health to be attained and maintained, the sexual rights of all persons must be respected, protected, and fulfilled."

There's a lot of information in that definition! Even with this great definition, it's important to recognize that sexual health is still individually defined. Your definition of sexual health might be different than another person's definition, and that's okay. The single common thread across all definitions is that for sexuality to be healthy, **it must be free of coercion**.

Some people believe that love, spirituality, and monogamy define healthy sexuality, but others may not subscribe to this same philosophy. Some believe that healthy sexuality may include alternative behaviors (e.g., same-sex encounters, anal sex, etc.), while others may find those behaviors disgusting. To get to **your** definition, let's begin by reviewing the CERTS Model of Healthy Sexuality developed by Wendy Maltz.

CERTS is an acronym that stands for:

Let's briefly define each of these.

Consent means that you can freely and comfortably choose whether or not to engage in sexual activity. In order to consent, you must be conscious, informed, and able to stop the activity at any time.

Equality is about the impact of uneven power dynamics on a sexual relationship, and how to address those uneven dynamics so that both people can feel comfortable regardless of the inequalities. Participants in a sexual encounter should have an equal voice and feel comfortable with the dynamics of the relationship.

Respect exists when you have positive thoughts, feelings, and attitudes towards yourself and your sexual partners. Participants in a sexual encounter should always feel their wishes are being honored by others.

Trust means that you are communicating with your sexual partner about any needs and vulnerabilities in the relationship, and you respond to those vulnerabilities with concern and sensitivity.

Safety is present in a sexual relationship when everyone involved feels comfortable with and assertive about where, when, and how the sexual activity takes place. Individuals must feel safe from the possibility of negative consequences such as unwanted pregnancy, sexually transmitted infections, and physical injury.

Now that you have a basic understanding of what constitutes sexual health, let's begin to examine your own definitions and how they may need to shift to better align with the CERTS model.

Reflect & Respond

1.   Let's start with the basics. In the box below, use the left column to list FIVE ideas that clearly fit YOUR definition of sexual health, and in the right column list FIVE ideas that clearly do not fit YOUR definition of sexual health.

2.   Do you believe you have ever experienced healthy sexuality? If so, when and what did it look like? If not, why not?

_____

_____

_____

Fits my Definition of Healthy Sexuality	Does Not Fit my Definition of Healthy Sexuality

3.   Review the CERTS model again. While reviewing it, are you able to see how child sexual abuse media cannot be healthy according to the CERTS model? Explain why below.

_____

_____

_____

Questions To Consider

Directions: Use the following questions to help develop your definition of healthy sexuality. When answering the questions, consider how each one may affect your plan for reaching and maintaining sexual health. If you have a significant realization, be sure to jot it down before you forget!

Do you identify as male/female/other? How does this affect your definition of sexual health?

Who are you sexually attracted to? What's their age? Their gender? What are some of their other attributes? How does this affect your definition of sexual health?

Who are you romantically attracted to? This may be different from who you are sexually attracted to.

How do these factors influence your attitudes toward sexuality? Think back to your Sexual Soup Recipe from earlier in this chapter.

- Religion
- Spirituality
- Ethics
- Family
- Culture
- Community
- Relationships
- Peers

Are there certain morals and values that are important to your sexuality?

What makes you feel sexually connected with others in a positive way?

What have your past sexual experiences been like? And what have you learned from these experiences? What would you like to repeat or not repeat from these experiences?

What sexual behaviors make you happy?

Are there sexual behaviors you want to try but are not sure about?

What thoughts or behaviors make your body feel good? (This good body feeling can be either a specific genital response or a more general positive bodily sensation.)

What sexual activities make you feel good about yourself?

What thoughts and behaviors make you feel sexually safe?

What boundaries will be important to follow in your definition of sexual health?

Are you able to communicate with others about your sexual emotions, fears, and concerns? Are you able to tell your sexual partner about these things?

What are the obstacles to achieving and maintaining your definition of sexual health?

Other than the physical aspects of sexual health, what other elements do you feel you should consider (e.g., sensuality, spirituality, physical health, etc.)?

What aspects of the CERTS Model of Sexual Health do you want to include in your definition of Sexual Health?

Remember the Seven Desires from Chapter 1? How do they fit into your sexual health plan?

React

It's time to create your own Definition/Vision of Sexual Health. We have developed a long list of questions to get you to think about your sexual thoughts, fantasies, and behaviors. Use the questions to guide you, but also know that it's ok to add to the questions if you think of things on your own. It's ok if you don't know all the answers... this is all a work in progress!

When creating your definition of healthy sexuality, you can use any type of design that works for you (a bulleted list, a circle or graph, a graphic or picture, etc.). Just be sure to place the words 'MY SEXUALITY' in the middle of your design. You may want to begin by revisiting Question #1 under Reflect & Respond above. Finally, be sure to ask your peers, your group, your therapist, or others for help as you work through the questions.

Notes

_____

_____

_____

_____

_____

_____

_____

_____

_____

_____

_____

_____

_____

_____

_____

Sexual Health Plan
Definition and Vision of Sexual Health

List, draw, illustrate, etc. your sexual health plan below.

True North Navigating Your Sexual Interest and Arousal

Everyone has a "True North" when it comes to sexual interest and arousal. Sexual interest and arousal are raw, immediate, and physical sensations. They are primal and should first be examined without the cultural influences of religion, family, morals, or values. You will add these cultural influences later, but let's forget them for this exercise.

On their own, sexual interest and sexual arousal are not right or wrong; they simply are. However, behaviors associated with our sexual interest and arousal can be abusive or hurtful, to both ourselves and others. And when that happens, it does make such behaviors wrong.

You might have trouble accepting your sexual interest and arousal. You may even experience guilt and shame when reflecting on your sexuality. The goal of this chapter is to help you view these aspects of yourself absent of all the "feelings" that might surface. Let's begin by answering some of the common questions individuals who view child sexual abuse media have about sexual interest and arousal.

What are the various types of sexual interest and arousal?

Everyone has their own unique sexual interest and arousal. There is no "standard" sexual interest or arousal. Many people have unusual aspects to their sexual interest and arousal that they often keep secret.

Are we born with our sexual interest and arousal?

There is some evidence that people are born with their sexual interest and arousal already set. However, there is also some evidence that sexual interest and arousal can be shaped by childhood experiences.

Can sexual interest and arousal be changed?

Professionals once thought that sexual interest and arousal were fully developed and unchangeable after adolescence. However, new research shows that the brain is more flexible and fluid than previously believed. To date, there is still a lot of debate about whether or not this brain flexibility is relevant to the area of sexual interest and arousal. Many experts feel it may be challenging to change a person's primary sexual interest and arousal, and others believe that only certain aspects of sexual interest and arousal may be changeable. Thankfully, most professionals agree that if your sexual interest and arousal template is problematic for you, it is possible to manage the sexual behaviors associated with your problematic sexual interest and arousal.

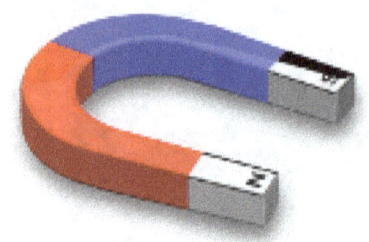

When does sexual interest and arousal become problematic?

Sexual interest and arousal can be problematic if you feel a tremendous amount of shame about who you are, since such shame often leads to acting out. Any acting out related to sexual interests that is abusive, illegal, or involves non-consenting sexual acts must be managed. Gaining awareness and managing the problematic aspects of sexual interest and arousal often requires consulting with professionals to help navigate all the complexities of the situation.

React

This exercise is designed to assist you in exploring your sexual interest and sexual arousal. It is important that you identify and "own" your sexual interest and arousal. The goal is to be as honest as you can about your sexual interest and arousal. Remember, no trained seals!

We are going to use the metaphor of a fire to help you identify your sexual interest and arousal template.

The bottom of the fire, where the wood is burning, represents the "hot zone." This is the zone where you are going to put types of people, fantasies, behaviors, and things that are most sexually attractive to you, those things that you are most aroused by. Be sure to include genders and ages of people, but not specific names of individuals. You should include the physical attributes of people you are most attracted to and aroused by, as well as any specific fantasies, behaviors, or things that are "really hot" for you.

The middle of the fire is the "warm zone." This is the zone where you will put the types of people, fantasies, behaviors, and things that you still find sexually attractive and arousing, but which are not "as hot" for you.

The top part of the bonfire is the "lukewarm zone." You may have some sexual interest or curiosity in the people, fantasies, behaviors, and things in this zone, but they don't necessarily "turn you on."

The sky above the bonfire represents your "cold zone." These are the people, fantasies, behaviors, and things that you are not sexually interesting or arousing to you.

Underneath the fire temperatures below, list your sexual interest and arousal zones.

Notes

_____

_____

_____

_____

_____

_____

COLD

LUKEWARM

WARM

HOT

Reflect & Respond

1. What surprises you as you look at your four zones?

    _____

    _____

    _____

2. Would your zones surprise those who know you well?

    _____

    _____

    _____

3. Do your zones include your viewing of child sexual abuse media? Where zone did this behavior fit into when you engaged in viewing this type of media. What zone does the behavior fit into now.

    _____

    _____

    _____

4. If engaging in the use of child sexual abuse media is not in your "hot zone" or "lukewarm zone" what caused the shift to a cooler zone for you?

    _____

    _____

    _____

The Thirteenth Witch

Adapted from the Sleeping Beauty Fairy Tale

Understanding difficult concepts can sometimes be easier when we use fables or fairy tales. When Sleeping Beauty was born, her family decided to hold a christening party and feast. However, the family had a dilemma: There were thirteen witches in the kingdom, and each needed a golden plate at the feast. Unfortunately, the family only had twelve golden plates, and there was no time before the feast in which to make a thirteenth golden plate.

The solution? The family decided to not invite the Thirteenth Witch. It was an easy decision, because the family didn't really like the Thirteenth Witch very much. The Thirteenth Witch was mean and scary and always caused problems at kingdom gatherings. When the Thirteenth Witch realized that she had not been invited to the christening party and the feast, she was very, very, very angry!

On the day of the christening party, all the witches came forward to bless Sleeping Beauty. After the Eleventh Witch had given her blessing, the uninvited Thirteenth Witch stormed into the feast, rageful for not being included (remember those Seven Desires.) She rushed up to Sleeping Beauty's cradle and cursed her to die.

The Twelfth Witch, who had not yet provided her blessing, said she could not undo the curse, but she could modify it so that Sleeping Beauty fell into a deep sleep until her Prince arrived.

Reflect & Respond

Try to answer the following questions before you read the paragraph at the end of the questions explaining this part of the Sleeping Beauty Fairy Tale

1. What do you think is the moral of this part of the Sleeping Beauty Fairy Tale?

    _____

    _____

    _____

2. How does this part of the Sleeping Beauty Fairy Tale relate to your sexuality?

    _____

    _____

    _____

3. What part of your sexuality is your Thirteenth Witch?

    _____

    _____

    _____

4. Based on the Sleeping Beauty Fairy tale what would be first step in addressing your Thirteenth Witch?

    _____

    _____

    _____

Don't Read this Box Until You Tried to Complete the Above Questions

Sleeping Beauty Explanation

The moral of the Sleeping Beauty Fairy Tale is that the thing which is ignored and disowned always comes back with a vengeance eventually. If you are not able to "own" and discuss all aspects of your sexual interest and arousal, then that interest and arousal will only grow stronger and more powerful. If you create a place at the metaphorical banquet for your unwanted sexual interest and arousal, you can keep an eye on them, get to know them, and learn to manage your unwanted sexual arousal and interest more effectively. Your Thirteenth Witch doesn't need to sit at the head table, but it does need to be invited to the party.

React

Back in Chapter 1, "Building the Foundations," you were asked to develop your "Inner Warrior." It's time to bring your Inner Warrior back, because they can help you with your Thirteenth Witch.

Inner Warriors have the strength to assist you in **understanding and owning** your sexual interest and arousal. Your Inner Warrior can give you the courage to overcome your shame and to **discuss** your sexual interest and arousal with your therapist, or other trusted people in your life. Finally, your Inner Warrior has the wisdom to allow you to better **manage** your Thirteenth Witch (aka your deviant sexual interest and arousal).

In the space below, create an image (drawing, collage, printed pictures, figurines, etc.) of your Inner Warrior and your Thirteenth Witch walking side by side. Under the image, write some dialogue about what the two would be saying to one another. After all, if you don't invite the Thirteenth Witch to talk with your Inner Warrior, how will you know what you are up against?

The Dark Side of the Brain: Understanding Deviant Sexual Fantasies

"Reality continues to ruin my life."

—Bill Watterson

We agree with Mr. Watterson's quote. Sometimes, reality sucks. Often, this makes us turn to a fantasy world to escape and feel better. There is certainly nothing wrong with that, so long as it is done in a healthy way. But our guess is your fantasy life has ended up finding ways to ruin things for you. Are we right?

Let's start with the basics. What is a sexual fantasy? It is more than just a sexual thought or image that quickly passes through the mind. Sexual fantasies are more complicated and elaborate. They often result in some type of sexual arousal (e.g., an erection) or a sexual behavior (e.g., masturbation, viewing pornography, sex with others, etc.).

Sexual Fantasies

Research tells us that most men and women have sexual fantasies. It is difficult to define what comprises a "normal" sexual fantasy because sexual fantasies vary wildly from person to person. For this workbook, we define a "deviant" sexual fantasy as one that focuses on underdeveloped (prepubescent or pubescent) children, or one that includes coercion.

Don't misunderstand. Sexual fantasies can be fun, entertaining, arousing, and pleasurable. Our goal is to help you enjoy a healthy sexual fantasy life, not to give it up. Healthy sexual fantasy might include erotic sexual elements or even "strange" fetish behavior. These fantasies are typically ok as long as the fantasy involves consenting sex among adults. However even sexual fantasies that involve consenting sex among adults may create guilt or shame which can then make the fantasies problematic for you. It is often complicated and difficult to figure out what is a healthy sexual fantasy because the answer is different for everyone.

Most people rarely discuss their sexual fantasies. It is a very personal and private part of one's life. But guess what? This workbook doesn't care about what "most people" do!

This exercise will encourage you to examine and share your fantasy world as a way to diminish the power and control that world can have over you. You may feel shame, guilt, disgust, or despair about your sexual fantasies – all the more reason to get them out of your head. As you seek to understand your deviant sexual fantasies, remember that our sexual fantasies can sometimes distract us from dealing with reality, or represent something we need in our lives – other than sex! Let's explore that a little.

The "Function" of Sexual Fantasies

All fantasies in our lives, including our sexual fantasies, serve a function. While sexual fantasies serve a sexual function (no big surprise there), often they also serve to distract us from our feelings, or from situations we may not want to face. These fantasies often provide use with "pseudo-relief for one or more of our Seven Desires (remember those?) that we are otherwise struggling to meet in our real life.

In sexual fantasies, people always *hear and understand* us, *affirm* us, *bless* us, *touch* us, *include* us, and make us *feel safe*. Sexual fantasies are a foolproof way to make ourselves feel better, if only for a moment, and to give us everything our heart desires.

When you have sexual fantasies that feel troubling, disturbing, or shameful, it is important to look underneath the sexual aspect of those fantasies to uncover what other functions they might be serving in your life. The following questions will help you with this exploration.

Notes

_____

_____

_____

Reflect & Respond

1. Do you experience sexual fantasies that feel troubling, disturbing, or shameful, and if so, how often do you experience these types of fantasies? What impact do they have on you?

    _____

    _____

    _____

2. Have you ever given any thought to the function sexual fantasies serve in your life, or do you instead find yourself automatically using sexual fantasies as a coping response without any further awareness?

    _____

    _____

    _____

3. What function do sexual fantasies have in your life? Do they distract you from negative feelings and/or situations? Do they meet one or more of your Seven Desires?

    _____

    _____

    _____

    _____

    _____

    _____

The next time you experience a sexual fantasy, try to "Iceberg Your Fantasy" (following page) to gain a better understanding of the fantasy's function. Continue to iceberg your sexual fantasies for the next month or so and jot some notes in the space below about what you have learned.

The Seven Desires Iceberg

The Big "M" Addressing Masturbation

Jacking off. Wanking. Beating off. Spanking the Monkey. Flying Solo. Fapping.

No matter what you call it, masturbation always seems to be a taboo subject that is not discussed. This workbook, however, is the place where it IS discussed! In 2018, more than 13,000 people from 18 different countries were surveyed about their masturbation habits. An average of 78% of males around the world admitted they masturbate… some weekly, some monthly, some less often, some more often.

Masturbation is the act of sexual self-stimulation resulting in erotic pleasure, arousal, or orgasm. The question often asked is, "Do I have a problem with masturbation?" That's a big question since the answer is "it depends." Most people ask that question with their frequency of masturbation in mind. But remember, some people believe any form of masturbation is unacceptable. They may hold that belief for moral or religious reasons, or perhaps they realize that, for them, masturbation routinely leads to dangerous behaviors. Alternatively, others might think masturbating multiple times a day is not a problem.

Is My Masturbation a Problem?

So, how do you know if YOUR masturbation is a problem? We recommend not focusing so much on frequency (although don't ignore it completely) and instead focusing more on the consequences of your masturbation. A common alcohol-use screening tool has been adapted below for your consideration:

C.A.G.E.

C - Have you tried unsuccessfully to **C**ut-Down on your masturbation activity because you were worried it was a problem?

A - Are other people **A**nnoyed with your masturbation? Perhaps a partner feels you can't perform because you masturbate too much? Perhaps you even feel this way yourself?

G - Do you feel **G**uilty after you masturbate, especially because you allowed masturbation to interfere with your life in some way? Romantically? Socially? Educationally? Occupationally? Or maybe in other ways?

E - Finally, do you need masturbation as an **E**ye-Opener or **E**ye-Closer? That is, do you need to masturbate to get a good night's sleep? Do you wake up in the morning and feel you need to masturbate to get your day going?

If you answered yes to ANY ONE of these questions, you might want to consider talking further with a professional about your masturbation concerns. You are likely not the best judge of whether you should begin to address your masturbation activity.

If you view child sexual abuse media while you masturbate, you are reinforcing a negative behavior that is not only illegal but victimizing to others. You will want to address these behaviors with your therapist and begin placing a safeguard around your pornography use as well as your masturbation.

What Can I Do?

If you decide that your masturbation is problematic for you, one thing to consider is a "Healthy Masturbation Plan." Like other plans outlined in this workbook, we suggest thinking in terms of a traffic light: green, yellow, and red. Below is an illustration of our suggested way of thinking about a healthy masturbation plan.

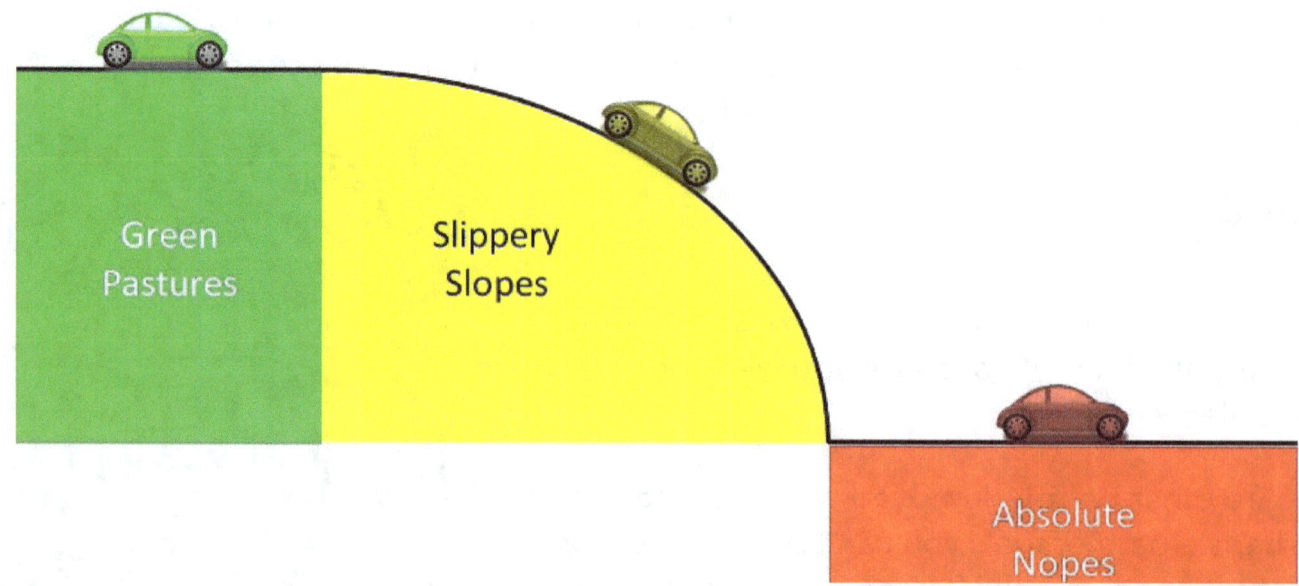

At the top left of the hill are the Green Pastures (green zone). This area represents masturbatory behaviors that are healthy and positive for you. Examples might include masturbating when thinking about adult, consensual relationships or when thinking about your partner. Masturbating in the green zone will not result in guilt, shame, or remorse. For those who may decide masturbation is never ok, the green zone can contain alternative behaviors to masturbating. These can include reaching out to others and going for coffee and contacting a sponsor or trusted friend.

The Slippery Slopes area (yellow zone) includes masturbatory behaviors that can lead directly into the Absolute Nopes (red zone). For example, some people realize that viewing or masturbating to online adult pornography is a slippery slope because, in the online world, it can only take seconds to go from viewing adult pornography to viewing child sexual abuse media. Masturbating when feeling lonely may be another slippery slope for some people.

Finally, there are the Absolute Nopes (red zone). You can list in this zone the masturbation behaviors that are NEVER ok for you… usually because you know they will result in significant emotional, physical, or legal consequences or are harmful to others. Examples include masturbating to child sexual abuse media, masturbating when you are in a certain emotional state (e.g., angry), masturbating in public, etc. Recognizing behaviors in this zone can help you to establish boundaries, so that you are clearly aware when you have crossed into behaviors that are not acceptable.

This masturbation plan should be created with the help of a trusted person, one who will be able to help you identify green, yellow, and red zone ideas that you might miss. It will also be important to revisit and revise this plan, at least once every couple of months, or perhaps even more often.

You may not always follow the plan, but once your plan is created, you will have a starting point for changing your behavior. It is difficult to engage in healthy masturbation if you don't have a starting point.

Reflect & Respond

1. Write a response to the CAGE questions below:

    C - Have you tried unsuccessfully to **C**ut-Down on your masturbation activity because you were worried it was a problem?

    _____

    A - Are other people **A**nnoyed with your masturbation? Perhaps a partner feels you can't perform because you masturbate too much? Others? Yourself?

    _____

    G - Do you feel **G**uilty after you masturbate, especially because you allowed masturbation to interfere with your life in some way? Romantically? Socially? Educationally? Occupationally? Other ways?

    _____

    E - Finally, do you need masturbation as an **E**ye-Opener or **E**ye-Closer? That is, do you need to masturbate to get a good night's sleep? Do you wake up in the morning and feel you need to masturbate to get your day going?

    _____

2. What roles has masturbation played in your life? Escape? Self-medication? Sexual Pleasure? Something else?

    _____

    _____

    _____

    _____

    _____

3. Have you masturbated while viewing child sexual abuse media? If so, describe the consequences, if any, that you experienced before, during, or after such behavior (e.g., guilt, shame, satisfaction, anxiety, power, depression, fear, etc.)?

_____

_____

_____

React

Use the following graphic to list your "Green Pastures," "Slippery Slopes," and "Absolute Nopes" related to your current masturbation habits. Revisit this completed Healthy Masturbation Plan again in two weeks to see if you think of other things to list. Also, share your plan with one trusted person to reduce your shame and get their input.

Turn the next page sideways to work on this activity. You will find a copy of this graphic on the workbook's companion webpage: www.internetbehavior.com/illegalimages

Notes

_____

_____

_____

_____

_____

_____

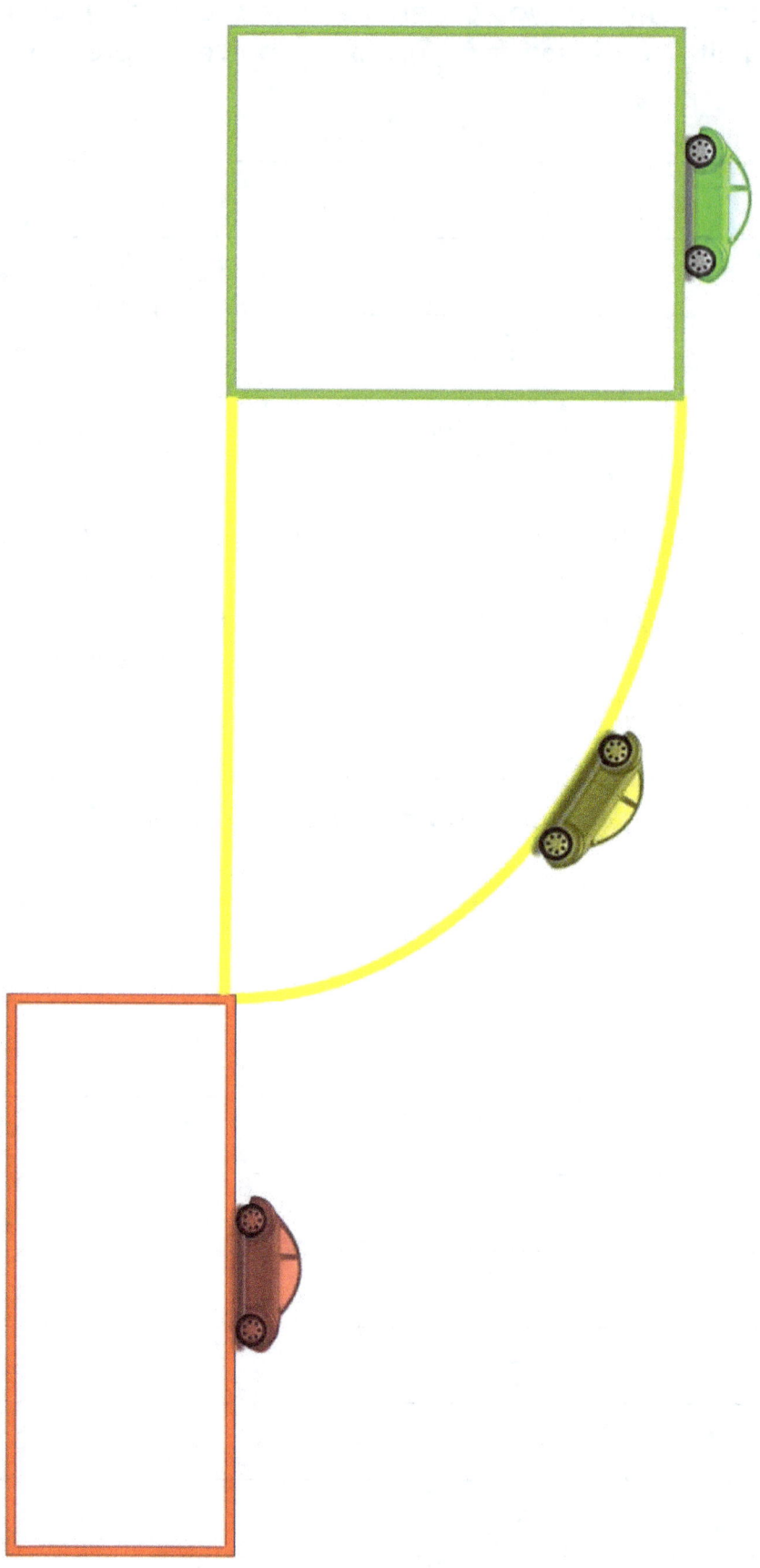

Two for the Price of One

We had two last ideas to provide and couldn't decide which one we should use. So, we have included both here. These two exercises offer practical suggestions on how to handle deviant thoughts, feelings, fantasies, or urges when they enter your mind. Sometimes you just need a couple extra tools in your toolbox when dealing with deviant thoughts, so we thought we should offer a couple here. We are hopeful they will help!

Exercise #1: Yo, Dude! Let's Ride the Urge Wave

What is an Urge?

The basic definition of an urge is "a mental impulse that persistently persuades someone to do something." In this exercise, we will be referring to an urge as your brain convincing you that you should engage in a specific behavior, despite the potential consequences of that behavior.

Some urges are biological. For example, I don't know about you, but as I get older, my bladder urges me to visit the bathroom more and more often. Or when you have a bad cold, your body often urges your lungs to expel mucus. But, in this exercise, we want you to think of non-biological urges, those that are "thought-driven."

…ok… now wait right here… I think I have to go to the bathroom.

Managing a Thought-Driven Urge

When you experience a thought-driven urge (referred to simply as an urge from now on), you likely respond in one of two ways: you either fight it or give in to it. However, there is a third approach called "Urge Surfing."

Urge surfing is the practice of riding out the urge and allowing it to pass naturally. You don't fight it. You don't ignore it. You don't give in to it. Instead, you acknowledge it, accept its presence, and let it gently pass over you.

No worries—we're offering free urge surfing lessons today!

Take a look at the following graphic:

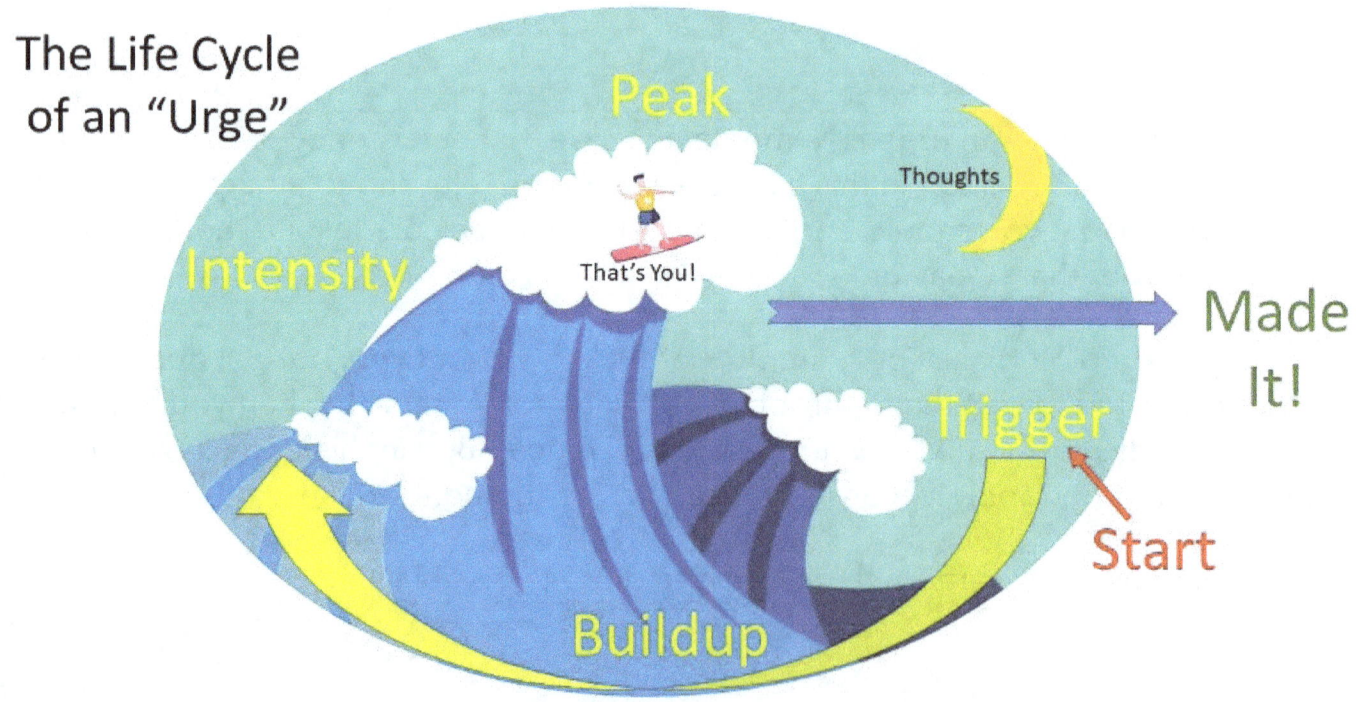

Surfing the Urge Wave

Urges typically begin with a trigger of some kind. It may stem from an emotion (e.g., feeling sad, angry, resentful, hopeless, etc.) or an event (e.g., an argument with your boss, seeing an attractive person, etc.). It can also arise from a deeper desire—to be heard and understood, to be affirmed, to be blessed, to feel safe, to be touched, to be chosen, or to be included (yes, those Seven Desires again!).

Once triggered, an "undercurrent" forms, setting the urge into motion. As it builds, your impulse to act out intensifies. If you pay attention to your body, you may feel this tension in your chest or stomach. You might even hear that small voice whispering that giving in will make you feel better.

As the urge gains strength, its intensity increases. Initially, it may feel like a mere craving or a passing desire, but in this phase, it transforms into what seems like an uncontrollable impulse. However, the reality is—you **always** have a choice!

Finally, the urge peaks! At this moment, you can either act on it or choose another path… you can ride it out. Our hope is that you **choose to ride it out!**

Our *Urge Life Cycle* graphic includes a crescent moon in the corner, symbolizing your thoughts. Just as the moon's gravitational pull affects the tide, your thoughts influence the intensity of your urges. You might catch yourself thinking, *"I can't do this," "I might as well give in to make it go away," "Nobody cares about me, so why should I care?"* or *"I deserve a break."*

These negative thoughts only make the urge waves stronger and harder to resist. But by shifting your mindset, you can learn to navigate them instead of being swept away.

During the buildup and intensity phases, your instinct may be to ignore the urge or push it away. Instead, we suggest a different approach—hop on your surfboard and ride it out. If you can ride the urge like a wave, it will crest, break, and eventually fade back into the ocean.

If you've ever tried surfing, you know it's not easy! Urge surfing isn't easy either, but here are five tips to help you get started:

1. Know that most urges last only about 30 minutes. Tell yourself to ride the wave in 15-minute increments. Set a timer and check in with yourself.

    _____

    _____

2. While distractions aren't necessarily the goal, they can be helpful. Keep a list of healthy activities to do while you ride out the wave.

    _____

    _____

3. Talk to the urge. Acknowledge and accept it. Tell it that you understand why it has appeared in your life, but you are choosing to do something else instead.

    _____

    _____

4. Urge surfing gets easier with practice. Just like learning to surf real waves, you may fall the first few times. Keep at it, and over time, you'll improve while the urges become less frequent and less intense.

    _____

    _____

5. Remember that community we've been encouraging you to build? Now's the time to activate it. Urges don't like exposure—so call someone, admit to the urge, and ask for support or suggestions on how to ride it out.

    _____

    _____

Final Tip: One of the best ways to manage urges is to prevent them from happening in the first place. Self-care (which is discussed throughout this workbook) is essential. Be sure to take care of your physical, emotional, social, and spiritual needs to prevent an "urge surge."

Reflect & Respond

1. Think back to the last urge you had. How did you address the urge? Were you able to ride it out, or did you end up acting impulsively? Write about what happened:

   _____

   _____

   _____

2. List several of your biggest triggers that lead to an urge. Remember, these might be feelings or situations that lead to a triggered state.

   _____

   _____

   _____

3. Which of the five tips listed above do you think will be most useful in surfing your next urge (choose as many as you need)? Can you think of other tips for yourself?

   _____

   _____

   _____

4. Reflect on the "moon thoughts" that have helped or hindered your control of the tide of your urge waves. On the left side of the chart below, list your negative thoughts that may be making your urge wave larger. On the right side, list positive thoughts that you can use to counteract your negative thoughts and make your urge surfing a little easier.

Negative Moon Thought	Counteracting Thought
_____	_____
_____	_____

React

The urge that is most important for you to surf through is your urge to use child sexual abuse media. Think back to the last time you used child sexual abuse media (or had the urge to use it) and complete the urge wave below. You may have to think hard about what preceded the use of the child sexual abuse media but do the best you can.

Trigger: _____

Buildup: _____

Intensity: _____

Peak: _____

Thoughts: _____

What Happened?: _____

If the "What Happened?" section mentions that you gave in to the urge, write some tips below that would have helped you ride the urge out better. If the "What Happened?" section indicates you did not engage in using child sexual abuse media, record what you did that made you successful so you can do it again next time.

_____

_____

_____

_____

_____

_____

_____

Urge Life Cycle

In the space below, create a visual representation of your Urge Life Cycle using the information above. Transforming words into an image will help you retain and understand the concepts!

Exercise #2: STOP, DROP, and ROLL

Do you remember when you were in elementary school and the firefighters came for a visit? They probably taught you that if you ever catch on fire, you should **STOP, DROP, and ROLL!**

Interestingly, those same words can be used to help manage unwanted, deviant sexual fantasies.

STOP - Whenever you experience an unwanted sexual thought—before it develops into a full fantasy—imagine a stop sign in your mind. Then, say out loud, **"STOP!"** If possible, yell it.

Some people wear a rubber band on their wrist or ankle and give it a quick *snap* to interrupt their thought process. Whatever it takes, **STOP** the thought from progressing. Then, distract yourself by physically moving to a different location and engaging in a new activity to shift your focus away from the sexual thought. This process is known as **thought stopping**.

DROP - If **STOP** doesn't work, then **DROP** into a healthier sexual fantasy to replace the deviant one. Reaching orgasm while focusing on deviant fantasies only reinforces their control. Therefore, it's important to shift to a healthier sexual fantasy as early as possible, as it becomes more difficult to change the fantasy the closer you are to orgasm.

ROLL - If you do reach orgasm while focusing on your deviant fantasy, you'll want to **ROLL** directly past the end of the fantasy and immediately begin imagining an alternative ending with a potential negative consequence. For example, picture yourself engaging in illegal sexual behavior as a result of the deviant fantasy—then imagine sitting in a jail cell, having to confess the fantasy to a loved one, or experiencing the shame and guilt that would follow if you acted on it.

Reflect & Respond

1. What other words or visuals could you use to help with the STOP part of the sequence? Examples might include NO! or a symbol like a stop light. Write your ideas below so you will have them in mind when you need them.

_____

_____

_____

2. Do you think it would be easy, difficult, or impossible for you to interrupt your deviant fantasy and replace it with a healthy one? Is there anything you could do to make it easier?

_____

_____

_____

_____

_____

_____

_____

3. When thinking about the ROLL part of the intervention process, what types of hypothetical consequences can you imagine happening as a result of the deviant fantasy you were having? Having these consequences in mind before the ROLL will help when the fantasy happens.

_____

_____

_____

Notes

_____

_____

_____

_____

_____

_____

_____

_____

_____

React

In order to **"DROP"** into a healthy sexual fantasy, you'll need to have a healthy sexual fantasy already in the bank, one that works for you and is stored and ready to go in your mind.

It's possible that you struggle with developing ideas about healthy sexuality. If so, writing a healthy sexual fantasy may be difficult for you, and you may need to seek out a therapist to help you with this exercise.

It may also help for you to look back at the "Healthy Sexuality" and "True North" exercises from earlier in this chapter. If you previously listed some appropriate "hot zone" and "warm zone" people, fantasies, behaviors, and things, be sure to incorporate those concepts into your healthy sexual fantasy.

Remember, your healthy sexual fantasy should be exciting, sexually arousing, and pleasurable to you! And also remember the elements of healthy sexuality discussed earlier in the chapter… Consent, Equality, Respect, Trust, and Safety.

You may want to include a detailed description of a past, present, or future partner that is sexually arousing to you. Include their age, physical attributes, and personality characteristics.

Also, as you create your sexual fantasy, think about the following questions:

What is your role in this sexual fantasy? Are you the pursuer, or are you being pursued? Do you take an active role in your sexual fantasy, or do you take a more passive role? What type of relationship do you have with your partner in your sexual fantasy? What sexual activities do you want to include in your sexual fantasy? Be specific and graphic.

In the space below, write out a healthy sexual fantasy that you can **"DROP"** into when needed. We encourage you to use this sexual fantasy when you masturbate, since reinforcing it with orgasm will solidify it.

Notes

_____

_____

_____

_____

_____

_____

_____

_____

_____

_____

_____

_____

_____

_____

Chapter 5: Out of Control Sexual Behavior

This chapter is centered around the feeling of being "out of control" with your sexual behavior. This feeling can have many different names including sex addiction, compulsive/impulsive sexuality, or problematic sexual behavior. But regardless of the various terminology used, the concept always refers to sexual behaviors that you feel you've lost some or all control over. Such behaviors may include the use of child sexual abuse media, masturbation, adult pornography, "hooking up" with casual partners, online chatting, and more. It is important to say that that even if you have engaged in these sexual behaviors, they may have felt problematic, but not out of control. This chapter will introduce you to information and exercises that can assist you in reflecting on whether or not your sexual behavior is or was out of control.

The exercises presented in this chapter will be useful for addressing general sexual behavior that may feel out of control but more importantly the information in this chapter will certainly help you better understand and address deviant sexual behavior that has become out of your control. Just think of it as a double-dipping bonus!

A List of Chapter Exercises

1. How Bad Is It, Doctor?
2. Zapping Your Cycle
3. I Can't Live Without You
4. Good Grief!
5. Porn Literacy
6. Driving Your Own Self-Care Bus
7. ATTACK PLAN!!!

Don't Forget!

Those who have access to the Internet may want to visit our companion website for resources related to this and other chapters in the workbook. These resources include additional articles, websites, and copies of activities/graphics from the chapters.

http://www.internetbehavior.com/illegalimages.

Notes

_____

_____

_____

_____

_____

_____

_____

_____

_____

How Bad Is It, Doctor?

This exercise is boring, but important. Below are three assessment tools that are commonly used in determining both the presence and the depth of someone's out of control online sexual behavior. Take each assessment by following the directions given. We suggest taking all three instruments concurrently, before attempting to score any of them.

One more note before you begin...If you have been working on managing your pornography use, masturbation, and other sexual behaviors you will likely score low on these tools. When responding to the assessments, we would like for you to think about a time when your sexual behavior was **at its worst**. This will help give you an idea of how problematic your sexual behavior became in your life. If you'd like, you can complete one assessment for when your behavior was at its worst, and one for today. This will allow you to compare your successes from the changes you have already made.

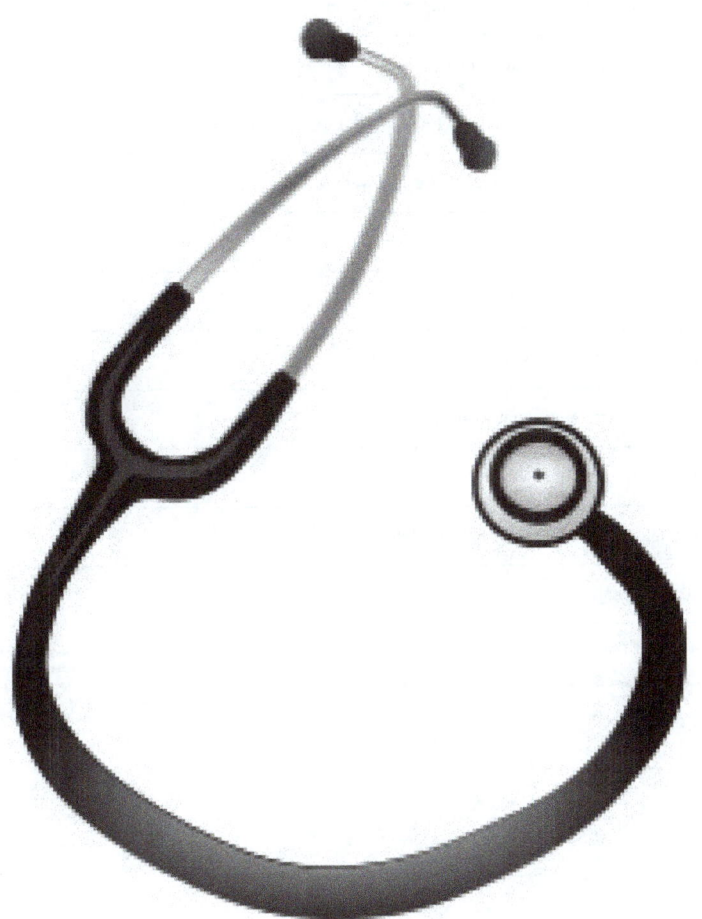

(HBI-19)

Below are a number of statements that describe various thoughts, feelings, and behaviors. As you answer each question, circle the number on the right that best describes you. Only circle one number per statement and please be sure to answer every question.

For the purpose of this questionnaire, sex is defined as any activity or behavior that stimulates or arouses a person with the intent to produce an orgasm or sexual pleasure. (e.g. self-masturbation or solo-sex, using pornography, intercourse with a partner, oral sex, anal sex, etc…) *Sexual behaviors may or may not involve a partner*.

Date:_____

ID #: _____

		Never	Rarely	Sometimes	Often	Very Often
1.	I use sex to forget about the worries of daily life.	1	2	3	4	5
2.	Even though I promised myself I would not repeat a sexual behavior, I find myself returning to it over and over again.	1	2	3	4	5
3.	Doing something sexual helps me feel less lonely.	1	2	3	4	5
4.	I engage in sexual activities that I know I will later regret.	1	2	3	4	5
5.	I sacrifice things I really want in life in order to be sexual.	1	2	3	4	5
6.	I turn to sexual activities when I experience unpleasant feelings (e.g. frustration, sadness, anger).	1	2	3	4	5
7.	My attempts to change my sexual behavior fail.	1	2	3	4	5
8.	When I feel restless, I turn to sex in order to soothe myself.	1	2	3	4	5
9.	My sexual thoughts and fantasies distract me from accomplishing important tasks.	1	2	3	4	5
10.	I do things sexually that are against my values and beliefs.	1	2	3	4	5
11.	Even though my sexual behavior is irresponsible or reckless, I find it difficult to stop.	1	2	3	4	5
12.	I feel like my sexual behavior is taking me in a direction I don't want to go.	1	2	3	4	5
13.	Doing something sexual helps me cope with stress.	1	2	3	4	5
14.	My sexual behavior controls my life.	1	2	3	4	5
15.	My sexual cravings and desires feel stronger than my self-discipline.	1	2	3	4	5
16.	Sex provides a way for me to deal with emotional pain I feel.	1	2	3	4	5
17.	Sexually, I behave in ways I think are wrong.	1	2	3	4	5
18.	I use sex as a way to try and help myself deal with my problems.	1	2	3	4	5
19.	My sexual activities interfere with aspects of my life such as work or school.	1	2	3	4	5

Rory C. Reid, Ph.D., Department of Psychiatry and Biobehavioral Sciences, University of California, Los Angeles
Sheila Garos, Ph.D., Psychology Department, Texas Tech University
Bruce N. Carpenter, Ph.D., Department of Psychology, Brigham Young University

Reid, R. C., Garos, S. & Carpenter, B. N. (2011). Reliability, validity, and psychometric development of the Hypersexual Behavior Inventory in an outpatient sample of men. *Journal of Sexual Addiction & Compulsivity, 18*(1), 30-51.

COPING: 1.3.6.8.13.16.18   CONSEQUENCES: 5.9.14.19   CONTROL: 2.4.7.10.11.12.15.17

Problematic Pornography Consumption Scale (PPCS-6)

When responding to the following statements, please think back to a time when your pornography use was at its highest and indicate on the 7-point scale about how often the statement applied to you. There is no right or wrong answer.

Keep in mind that pornography is defined as material (text, picture, video, etc.) that (1) creates or elicits sexual feelings or thoughts and (2) contains explicit exposure or descriptions of sexual acts involving the genitals, such as vaginal or anal intercourse, oral sex, or masturbation.

Problematic Pornography Consumption Scale (PPCS-6)

1=Never / 2=Rarely / 3=Occasionally / 4=Sometimes / 5=Often / 6=Very Often / 7=All the Time	
I felt that porn is an important part of my life.	1 2 3 4 5 6 7
I released my tension by watching porn.	1 2 3 4 5 6 7
I neglected other leisure activities as a result of watching porn.	1 2 3 4 5 6 7
I felt that I had to watch more and more porn for satisfaction.	1 2 3 4 5 6 7
When I vowed not to watch porn, I could only do it for a short period of time.	1 2 3 4 5 6 7
I became stressed when something prevented me from watching porn.	1 2 3 4 5 6 7
	Total Points: _____ (min=6 / max=42)

Internet Sex Screening Test

Directions: Read each statement carefully. If the statement is mostly TRUE, place a check mark on the blank next to the item number. If the statement is mostly false, skip the item and place nothing next to the item number. Respond to each item while thinking about a time when your online sexual behavior was at its worst. When you read "online sexual media" this means pornography. When you read the word "sex" please think broadly to include sex with others, sex with self, viewing pornography, etc.

___ 1. I have saved/favorited/liked online sexual media.

___ 2. I spend more than 8 hours per week using an electronic device for sexual pursuits.

___ 3. I have spent money associated with online sexual media (pornography, streaming, tips, or wishlist gifts, etc.).

___ 4. I have livestreamed myself for sexual purposes.

___ 5. I have searched for sexual material through an Internet search tool.

___ 6. I have spent more money for online sexual media than I planned.

___ 7. Online sex has interfered with certain aspects of my life (e.g., relationships, education, work, etc.)

___ 8. I have participated in sexually related messaging (chats, phone texting, etc.).

___ 9. I have a sexualized username, nickname, gamertag, etc. that I use online.

___10 I have masturbated while using my devices for sexual purposes.

___11 I have accessed sexual media from my workplace or during a time I should be working.

___12 No one knows I use my electronic devices for sexual purposes.

___13 I have tried to hide what is on my electronic device so others cannot see it.

___14 I have stayed up after midnight to access sexual media online.

___15 I use the Internet to experiment with different aspects of sexuality (e.g., bondage, homosexuality, anal sex, etc.)

___16 I have created online sexual content for others to view (e.g., selfies, website, streaming, etc.)

___17 I have made promises to myself to stop using my electronic devices for sexual purposes.

___18 I sometimes use online sex as a reward for accomplishing something. (e.g., finishing a project, stressful day, etc.)

___19 When I am unable to access sexual media online, I feel anxious, angry, or disappointed.

___20 I have increased the risks I take online with others for sexual purposes (give out name and phone number, meet people offline, viewing illegal media, etc.)

___21 I have punished myself when I go online for sexual purposes (e.g., time-out from electronic devices, cancel subscriptions, etc.)

___22 I have used hookup apps or other methods to connect with people offline in order to have sex with them.

___23 I enjoy trolling or bullying others while online.

___24 I have seen illegal sexual media (child pornography) while online.

___25 I believe I am an online sex addict.

___26 I have repeatedly attempted to stop or cut-back my online sexual behavior, but have failed.

___27 I continue to engage in online sexual behavior even though it has caused me problems.

___28 After engaging in online sexual behaviors I often feel regret, guilt and/or shame.

___29 I have often lied to others in order to conceal my online sexual behaviors.

___30 I have joined public or private groups whose sole purpose is to trade sexual media.

___31 I worry about people finding out about my online sexual behavior.

___32 I enjoy playing video games that have a significant amount of sexual content.

___33 I was exposed to online sexual media prior to the age of 12 years old.

___34 I feel depressed after I engage in online sexual behaviors.

___35. I have used artificial intelligence (AI) or virtual reality (VR) to engage in online sexual behavior.

There, wasn't that fun? If you are reading this, you should have completed all three tests. If not, STOP, go back, and complete the tests! Next, we will discuss each test separately, explaining what the test measured, how to score it, and what the results might mean for you.

Hypersexual Behavior Inventory

The Hypersexual Behavior Inventory (HBI) measures what is called "hypersexuality." That's just a fancy word for out of control sexual behavior. The HBI is not specific to the Internet and scores may indicate problems with both online and offline sexual behaviors. The author of this inventory, Dr. Rory Reid, has graciously given permission to use the HBI with clients…thanks Rory!

Scoring the HBI is easy. Simply add up the numbers you circled on the page for all nineteen items. If you circled a five, give yourself five points, if it's a three, then three points. A calculator may be helpful. Your score should fall between 19 and 95.

Once you have a total score, plot it on the line below. Use the following guidelines. If your score is:

      <47 - place a star to the far left of the line
      47 - 50 - place a star in the green area
      50 - 53 - place a star in the yellow area
      53 - 56 - place a star in the red zone
      56+ - place a star to the right of the line

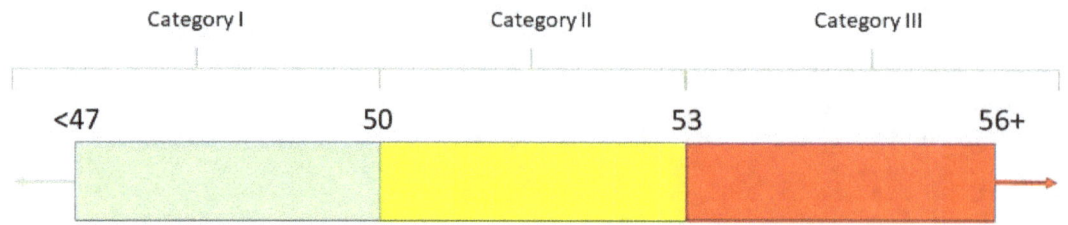

Look above the line for the corresponding category. You will fall into one of three categories.

Category I: Lower risk for out of control sexual behavior

Category II: At-risk for out of control sexual behavior

Category III: Meets criteria for out of control sexual behavior

The interpretation is fairly self-explanatory. Individuals in Category I are not free from risk but scored more similarly to those who do not have out of control sexual behavior. Those in Category II are considered to be at a higher risk for developing out of control sexual behavior. Finally, those in Category III have already crossed the cutoff score and are considered to be out of control with their sexual behavior.

Problematic Pornography Consumption Scale (PPCS-6)

The Problematic Pornography Consumption Scale (PPCS-6) is a six-item scale that measures problematic pornography use. Research indicates it is a valid and reliable measure of problematic pornography use. It can successfully separate individuals who have problematic pornography use from those who do not. The PPCS-6 is a shorter version of the 18-item, full-scale Problematic Pornography Consumption Scale, but it has been found to be as good as the longer instrument. Permission was given by Beata Bőthe to use the PPCS-6 in this workbook…thanks Bea!

To score the PPCS-6, simply total up your ratings for the six items. Since the rating scale is 1 to 7 and there are six items, your score should be no less than 6 and no more than 42. Place a large "X" on the number line below to represent your score.

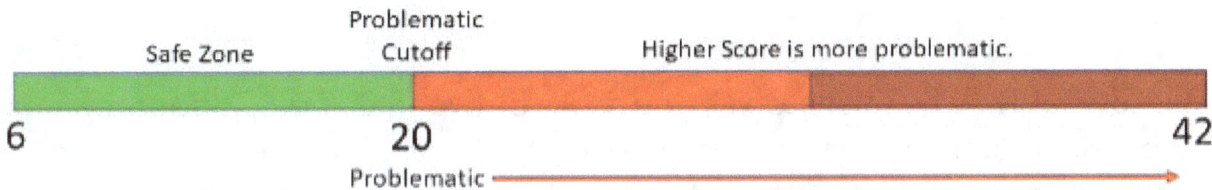

The cutoff score for problematic pornography use on PPCS-6 is 20 points. As your score gets higher, the more problematic your pornography viewing is likely to be. Scores between 6 and 19 are considered "safe" on this tool, but still should be monitored closely.

Internet Sex Screening Test (slightly modified)

The Internet Sex Screening Test was developed by David Delmonico and Elizabeth Griffin (that's us!) in response to the fact that there were no valid and reliable assessment tools specifically for online sexual behavior. After collecting data from more than 5,000 people, the ISST was developed to screen for out of control sexual behavior.

To score the assessment, simply add up the number of TRUE statements on the test. There are 35 items, so the possible scores range from 0 to 35. Once you have your score, you can use the graphic below to interpret it. Look on the right side of the graphic to find the "block" that represents your score, then look to the left of that block to see the interpretation. I know, I know… green, yellow, red again!

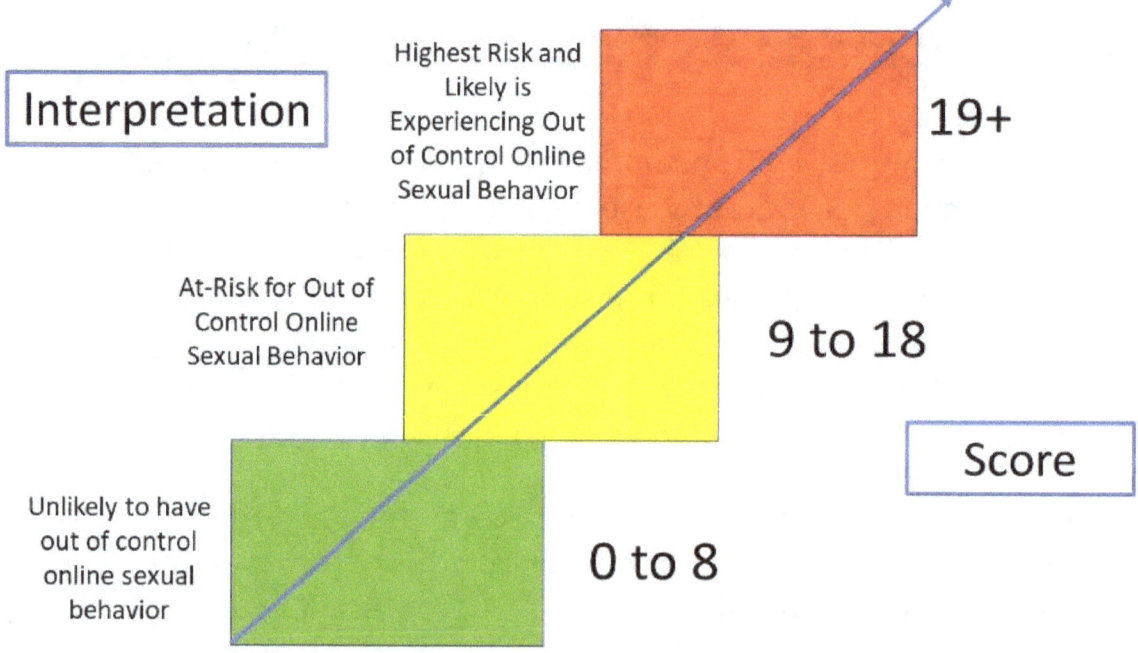

The results are fairly self-explanatory. If you score between 0 and 8, it does not appear that your online sexual behavior is "compulsive"; however, that does not equate to it not being problematic. Scores between 9 and 18 is a "danger zone" and you should keep an eye on your online sexual behavior becoming even more problematic and compulsive. Finally, scores about 19 are indicative of online out of control sexual behavior. As such, you may need some extra help from a professional to address this issue.

Reflect & Respond

1. Now that you have completed all three tests, study the results of each. Did the assessments all match in their interpretation? If so, the results are more trustworthy. What are some observations you have from taking the testing and the results?

    _____

    _____

    _____

2. Were there any big surprises in the results of the testing that you had not considered before?

    _____

    _____

    _____

3. What do you want to do with this data now that you have it? Share it? Hide it? Think on it? Shred it? Embrace it? How will knowing this information help you to move forward?

    _____

    _____

    _____

React

Surprise! There is no REACT to this exercise. The React was to take the assessment tools. Does it feel like your teacher just gave you a night off from homework? Yahoo!

Zapping Your Cycle

It is important to understand the theory behind how and why people develop and sustain out of control online sexual behavior. You may find that you share a common background and characteristics with others who struggle to control their behaviors – sexual and otherwise.

The following graphic shows how most professionals believe the cycle of being out of control begins and is sustained over time. This includes alcohol, drug use, gambling, sexual behavior, and other out of control behaviors.

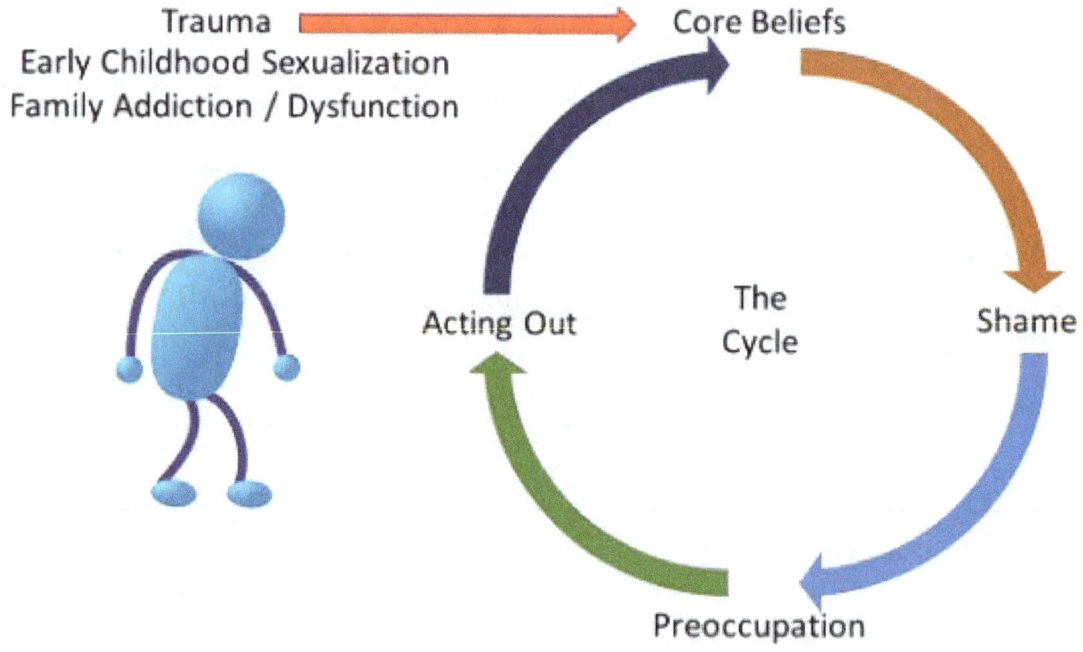

The theory is that trauma, early childhood sexualization, and/or some type of family dysfunction "activates" and "feeds" the system. Once the system is activated, the cycle begins and continues. It is very difficult to break out of a cycle once it has been activated.

Let's review what happens in the cycle:

Core Beliefs. Once the cycle is activated, the first thing that happens is you begin to create negative beliefs about yourself (usually on a subconscious level). These negative core beliefs typically begin appearing during childhood and are then carried on throughout a person's lifetime.

Examples of core beliefs that feed into the addiction cycle include:

I am not good enough (inadequate, less than, etc.)
I am a bad person.
I am unworthy of love.
I am unable to tolerate life.
I am a failure.
I am a burden to others.

One of the main problems with core beliefs like these is that they become the driving force behind how you live your life. That means that you live every day trying to find evidence that supports these core beliefs so you can tell yourself, "See, it's true!" even when there is a lack of evidence to support it. You may even begin seeking out actions that prove to yourself it is true – we call this behavior a "self-fulfilling prophecy."

Shame. When you repeat your core beliefs enough, you begin to believe they are true and feel shameful about who you are as a person. Brené Brown, an author and researcher specializing in shame and vulnerability, writes that shame is an intensely painful feeling or experience of believing that we are flawed and, therefore, unworthy of love and belonging. We believe that something we've experienced, done, or failed to do makes us unworthy of connection with others. Shame is one of the most critical aspects of the cycle for you to examine.

What about guilt? Is that the same as shame? No. Shame is derived from negative messages that the world has told us or that we have told to ourselves about being "bad." It results in being made to feel "less-than" our peers. Guilt is instead something we feel when we have harmed someone, and it is often accompanied by a desire to make amends to that specific person.

Preoccupation. The purpose of preoccupation is to distract us from our shame. We obsess about how to escape the intolerable sense of shame we feel as part of the cycle.

One of the ways to tell if you are in the preoccupation stage of your cycle is to look at rituals you might use to prepare for your online sexual behaviors. There is a great deal of anxiety in the preoccupation stage and rituals are one way to reduce anxiety. These rituals might start minutes, hours, days, or even weeks before you actually act out. Identifying them will be the first step in addressing your preoccupation.

Examples of rituals include:

> *It's Monday and you are already planning how to get time for yourself to engage in online sexual behaviors over the next weekend.*

> *Preparing the setting (car, house, work, etc.) where you plan to act out to make it conducive to your online sexual behaviors.*

> *Planning a certain time to act out (after midnight, when your partner goes to bed, first thing in the morning, etc.)*

> *You always pour yourself a drink (alcoholic or non-alcoholic) or get yourself a snack before sitting down with your device, etc.*

> *You grab toilet paper, tissues, a towel, an old sock, etc. that you plan to use for masturbation.*

Acting Out. This seems self-explanatory, but there are many ways to act out. Obviously, using child sexual abuse media is one way (or other online pornography, sexualized chat, etc.), but you may have other ways of acting out. Maybe you act out with your eating behavior? Maybe you use rage to control others? Those extra alcoholic beverages? That's right, acting out.

Acting Out comes in many forms. It's just some forms are more obvious than others.

Final Note: Not all professionals subscribe to this model of understanding out of control behaviors, but after 30+ years in the field, we believe it is the most common way for such behavior to occur. Of course, there are always exceptions.

Reflect & Respond

1. How does the cycle of out of control behavior discussed in this exercise fit for you? Or how does it not fit for you?

_____

_____

_____

2. What are some of the core beliefs that you have identified in your life? Do you think that any of them feed into your cycle of out of control sexual behavior?

_____

_____

_____

3. Other than your online sexual acting out behavior, what are some other ways that you act out?

_____

_____

_____

4. Who are the support people in your life that can help you identify the different aspects of your cycle and help you identify others ways you act out?

_____

_____

_____

Today, you are being hired as a reverse electrician. Most electricians want to prevent or fix short circuits, but we are asking you to create them. All the moving parts in a cycle make it complex. However, the good thing is that if you make a positive change in one part, all the other parts of the cycle can also experience a positive change.

Below we have included another illustration of the cycle of out of control online sexual behavior, except this time, there are screwdrivers between each of the stages. Notice they are numbered. These screwdrivers are from your electrician's tool belt. We are asking you to stick those metaphorical screwdrivers into your cycle and zap the circuit. (Be Careful!)

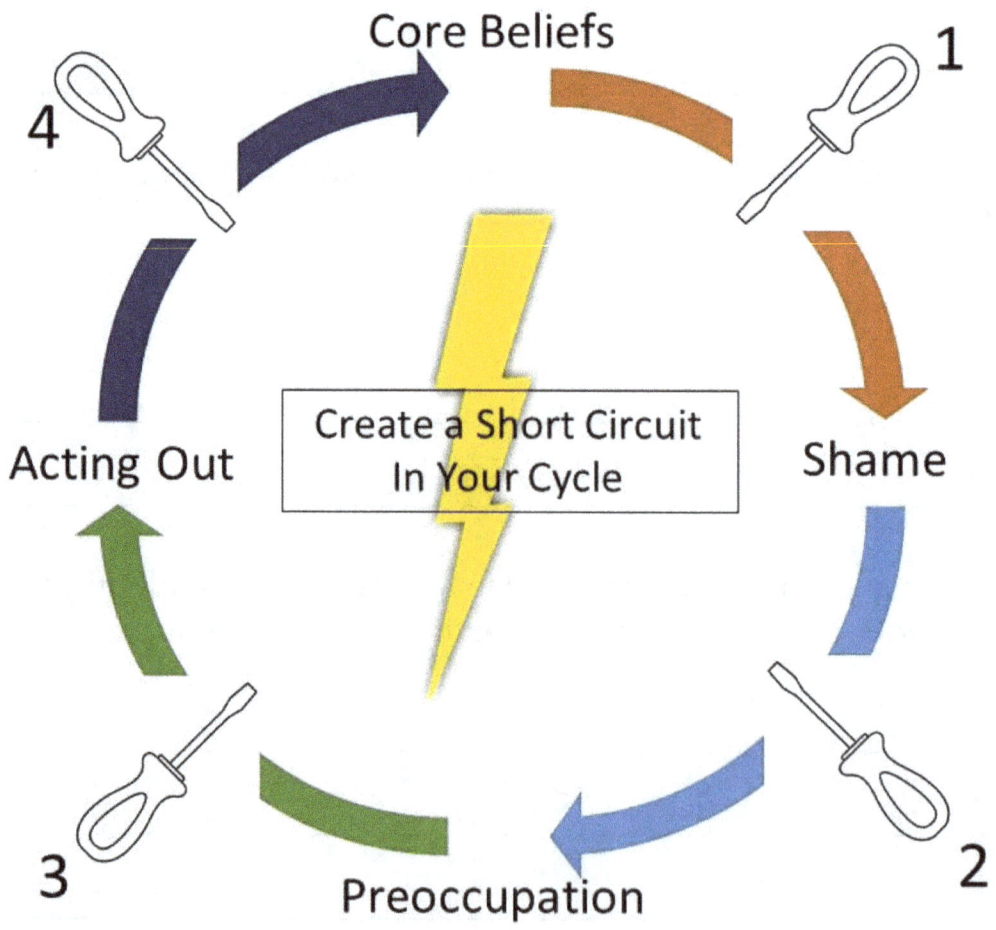

The point here is that you need to develop skills and strategies to break the cycle. You can do that by addressing any part of the cycle, including your core beliefs, your shame, your preoccupation, or your acting out. By addressing just one of these areas, the other areas will also improve, and the cycle will eventually be broken.

Right now, see what ideas you have for short-circuiting your cycle without any more help from us. Then, later in this chapter, we will provide you with some more skills and tools that will be helpful in short-circuiting your cycle.

Screwdriver #1: This screwdriver sits between your core beliefs and the shame that you are allowing those beliefs to develop. What data do you have to support that your core beliefs are true? Would others say the same things about you that you say to yourself? Write below how you can begin to address and change your core beliefs.

_____

_____

_____

_____

_____

Screwdriver #2: Now it's time to examine what happens between your shame and preoccupation. Think about what role shame plays in your life. How does it keep you stuck? How does it lead to more problems? Those who struggle with child sexual abuse media often feel a great deal of shame about themselves. What are some shame-reducing actions you can take to avoid the preoccupation and ritualization that may come next? Hint: You may need others to help reduce your shame.

_____

_____

_____

_____

Screwdriver #3: We are getting closer to acting out. The preoccupation and rituals have started. Now what? Of course, "noticing" is the first step. Then, how can you change the rituals? And how can you involve others in short-circuiting them? After all, you know where you're headed if you don't do something about it! You are in a DANGER Zone! Get out! But, how?

_____

_____

_____

_____

_____

Screwdriver #4: Ok, unfortunately, despite your best efforts, everything you have done so far has not prevented you from acting out. Either you can sulk and start the cycle all over again, or you can revisit what happened and make some changes. If you do nothing at all with your relapse, you will simply reinforce your core belief that you are a loser and begin everything all over again. Aren't you tired of this? List some questions below that you can ask yourself if you get into the red zone or have acted out in some way. This screwdriver won't work if you just allow your acting out to reinforce your core beliefs.

_____

_____

_____

_____

_____

I Can't Live Without You

Abstinence. It's a word that can strike fear into the hearts of those with out of control sexual behaviors. After all, most of you are not priests. You didn't take a vow of celibacy. So why on earth would you stop engaging in all sexual behaviors for any particular period of time? Well, this exercise may help to convince you that an abstinence plan is not a punishment, and that such a plan may in fact be helpful on your sexual healing journey.

Why Abstinence?

A **period** of sexual abstinence is often recommended by professionals who work with individuals with out of control sexual behavior. Notice we bolded the word "period." We are not suggesting that you never engage in sex again, we are just suggesting you consider a **period** of abstinence. More about this later in the exercise!

One of the goals of abstinence is to help you "detox" from sex and take time re-assessing your sexual behaviors, distinguishing between those behaviors that are healthy and those that are unhealthy. Obviously, using child sexual abuse media is an unhealthy behavior which you should always avoid.

Engaging in a period of sexual abstinence means giving up any behavior intended to result in sexual arousal. This includes sex with others, intentional sexual fantasies, masturbation, viewing pornography, engaging in fetishes, etc. Keep in mind that sexual arousal does not always result in an erection… sexual arousal may simply be the sexual feelings you have, even in the absence of an erection.

An abstinence period can serve as a "reset" for individuals who feel their sexual behavior has taken control of their lives. The decision to enter into a period of sexual abstinence is one that should be made with careful thought and consideration. If you are in counseling or attend a group, it would be wise to discuss what sexual abstinence will look like for you. Abstinence requires preparation and support from others.

Preparing for Abstinence

During the time of sexual abstinence, intense feelings may surface. For many of you, sex has served as a way to avoid dealing with your feelings, or even to escape from them entirely; therefore, the abstinence period may result in a flood of feelings and memories that you have previously locked away. You may experience frustration, anger, resentment, etc. For this reason, an abstinence period is not a good idea until you have support and community! We do not recommend entering into an abstinence period until you have the support of others.

A typical abstinence period is 90 days. Again, this means no masturbation, no viewing pornography, and no engaging in any behaviors (online or offline) that result in sexual arousal. What was your first thought when hearing this? Was it, "OMG! There is no way I can go 90 days without sex!" If so, an abstinence contract is for you! 🙂 Some people decide to try a 30-day period of abstinence to see how it feels. They may extend it once they realize they can handle it.

It's likely that an abstinence period is good for anyone reading this workbook. You can use the abstinence time to reflect on your sexuality and even complete or revisit some of the exercises in this book with a clear mind. Your Sexual Health Plan (discussed later in this chapter) may look very different during a period of abstinence rather than if you completed it when you were when you were engaging in sexual activities.

Here are some steps before starting an abstinence period:

1.   Be sure you have someone to support you during this period (e.g., therapist, sponsor, support person, group, etc.)

2.   Choose a length of time for the abstinence contract. We suggest either 30, 60, or 90 days.

3.   Purchase a new journal or diary to take notes and observe your thoughts and feelings during the abstinence period.

4.   Discuss your plans with your support people mentioned in step #1.

5.   Create a list of coping strategies and leisure activities you can use to manage any difficult thoughts, feelings, or urges that may surface during the abstinence period.

Some Final Thoughts

Abstinence for people who struggle with out of control sexual behavior is different from abstinence for other out of control behavior. The goal for those with substance use issues is permanent abstinence… that is *NOT* your goal here. Your goal in this case is to develop a healthy sense of sexuality that you can return to after your abstinence period is over.

Some people start their abstinence period and decide it is easier just to avoid sex altogether; however, this can result in "sexual anorexia." Sexual anorexia is a term that was made popular by sex addiction expert Dr. Patrick Carnes. Dr. Carnes used the term to describe compulsive avoidance of sex. In his book, *Sexual Anorexia: Overcoming Sexual Self-Hatred*, Dr. Carnes writes that sexual anorexia is simply another form of out of control sexual behavior because it just represents the opposite side of the same coin.

When people "flip" to the sexually anorexic side of the coin, they often avoid any sexual contact, sexual pleasure, or even emotional intimacy for fear that it will lead to sexual acting out. People often feel "more in control" during an anorexic phase. However, remember sexual anorexia is as problematic as sexual acting out. The tight control of shutting down your sexuality will eventually cause you to "flip" back into sexual acting out. You'll receive extra credit if you can use Hermes' Web (discussed in Chapter 1, "Building the Foundation") to think about this dynamic and explain it to your therapist or support person.

What If I Fail?

There is no such thing as failing in this exercise. This exercise is not about shaming you into doing something different, rather it is about creating an opportunity to learn more about yourself.

If you don't make it until the end of your abstinence contract, consider what you have learned. Perhaps you'd like to try again? Perhaps it can wait. See what your support people say about it and journal about what you learned about yourself during the process.

Reflect & Respond

1. How do you feel about the possibility of engaging in an abstinence period? Too scary? Too restrictive? I don't need it!? Will it be a relief?

_____

_____

_____

_____

_____

2. What would be **YOUR** pros and cons of engaging in an abstinence period?

Yay! Abstinence! (Pros)	OMG! NO!!!! (Cons)

3. What period of time would you choose for your abstinence period, and why did you choose that amount of time?

_____

_____

_____

4. What's your understanding of the difference between abstinence and sexual anorexia?

_____

_____

_____

5. Have you ever experienced a period of sexual anorexia? What caused it? How did you get out of it?

_____

_____

_____

React

Obviously, we recommend trying out an abstinence period or we would not have included this exercise for you to consider. This mission, should you choose to accept it, can be undertaken by completing the "Abstinence Contract" on the next page, which will symbolize and detail your commitment to the abstinence period. You will notice that the "contract" asks for both your signature and the signature of someone else you have discussed your intentions with. This person can serve as an accountability/support person for you.

Notes

_____

_____

_____

_____

_____

_____

_____

_____

Abstinence Contract

Name: _____

Date: _____

Abstinence Period:

     ☐ 30 Days   ☐ 60 Days   ☐ 90 Days   ☐ Other _____

   ☐ I have a journal/diary

   ☐ I have a support team in place

By signing this contract, I agree to make a significant effort in abstaining from all forms of sexual arousal (e.g., intentional sexual fantasy, masturbation, sexual contact with others, viewing pornography in all forms, online sexual behavior such as chatting or using AI bots, etc.).

I understand that abstinence may bring up emotional and behavioral challenges. Therefore, I have made a plan to help cope with these thoughts, feelings, and urges by listing coping strategies, leisure activities, and support people.

Coping & Leisure Strategies	Support Team
1._____	1._____
2._____	2._____
3._____	3._____
4._____	4._____
5._____	5._____

_____   _____

Signature   Support Person Signature

Good Grief!

Do you know why the concept of grief is closely related to out-of-control sexual behavior? The connection stems from the fact that, while out-of-control sexual behavior often creates many problems in a person's life, it can also feel like a "warm and fuzzy" blanket for some individuals. The reality for many is that their out-of-control sexual behavior has been a consistent source of comfort, shielding them from painful memories or emotions. Therefore, it is natural for them to experience grief when giving up a familiar and well-used coping strategy.

Additionally, while grieving the loss of out-of-control sexual behavior, individuals may also recognize the losses they have previously experienced due to their behavior. Acknowledging these losses can be a source of profound grief.

What Exactly is Grief?

Grief is a natural and normal reaction to loss and change. It occurs when something or someone we depend on is no longer present. Grief is a process that takes time to work through. The first step in addressing grief is to recognize and understand what is happening.

Elisabeth Kübler-Ross, a prominent Swiss-American psychiatrist, described the five stages of grief in her book, *On Death and Dying*. The five stages she identified were, in order: denial, anger, bargaining, depression and acceptance.

If you struggle with out of control sexual behavior, you may say to yourself, "As long as my sexual behavior is not illegal, maybe I don't have to give it up? It is not really hurting me or anyone else." This is the **denial** stage.

When you begin to realize that you may have to give up your out of control sexual behavior, you might become angry. You might say to yourself, "Other people can look at adult pornography, I should be able to look at it too! Or why can't I chat sexually with others... it's not like an affair! This just isn't fair!" This is the **anger** stage.

When you start to say, "What if I just look at a little adult pornography? What if I just look at adult pornography on the weekends? What if I just look at pictures of children in swimsuits?" This is the **bargaining** stage.

When you start to realize that you really have to give up certain sexual behaviors that are out of control in your life, the **depression** stage begins.

When you accept that you have a problem, that your sexuality does not match the person you want to be, and that you need to make changes, you enter the **acceptance** stage.

The Art of Kintsugi

Have you heard of Kintsugi? It is the Japanese art of repairing broken pottery with gold—built on the idea that by embracing flaws and imperfections, we create something even stronger and more beautiful.

Every break in a piece of pottery is unique, and rather than trying to make the object look as if it was never broken, this 400-year-old technique highlights its "scars" as part of its design.

Sometimes, in repairing what has been broken, we create something more unique, beautiful, and resilient.

This is our hope for you as you address your use of child sexual abuse media.

React #1

On the next page, you will find a large circle with arrows pointing both toward and away from its center.

In the middle of the circle, write the words "Out of Control Sexual Behavior."

On the blue arrows pointing into the circle, write words and phrases that describe how your out-of-control sexual behavior has helped you cope with your life in the past. For example, it may have helped you avoid doing things you didn't want to do or allowed you to escape stressful situations.

On the red arrows pointing away from the circle, write words and phrases that describe what out-of-control sexual behavior has taken from your life. Has it put your relationships in jeopardy? Your employment? Even your freedom?

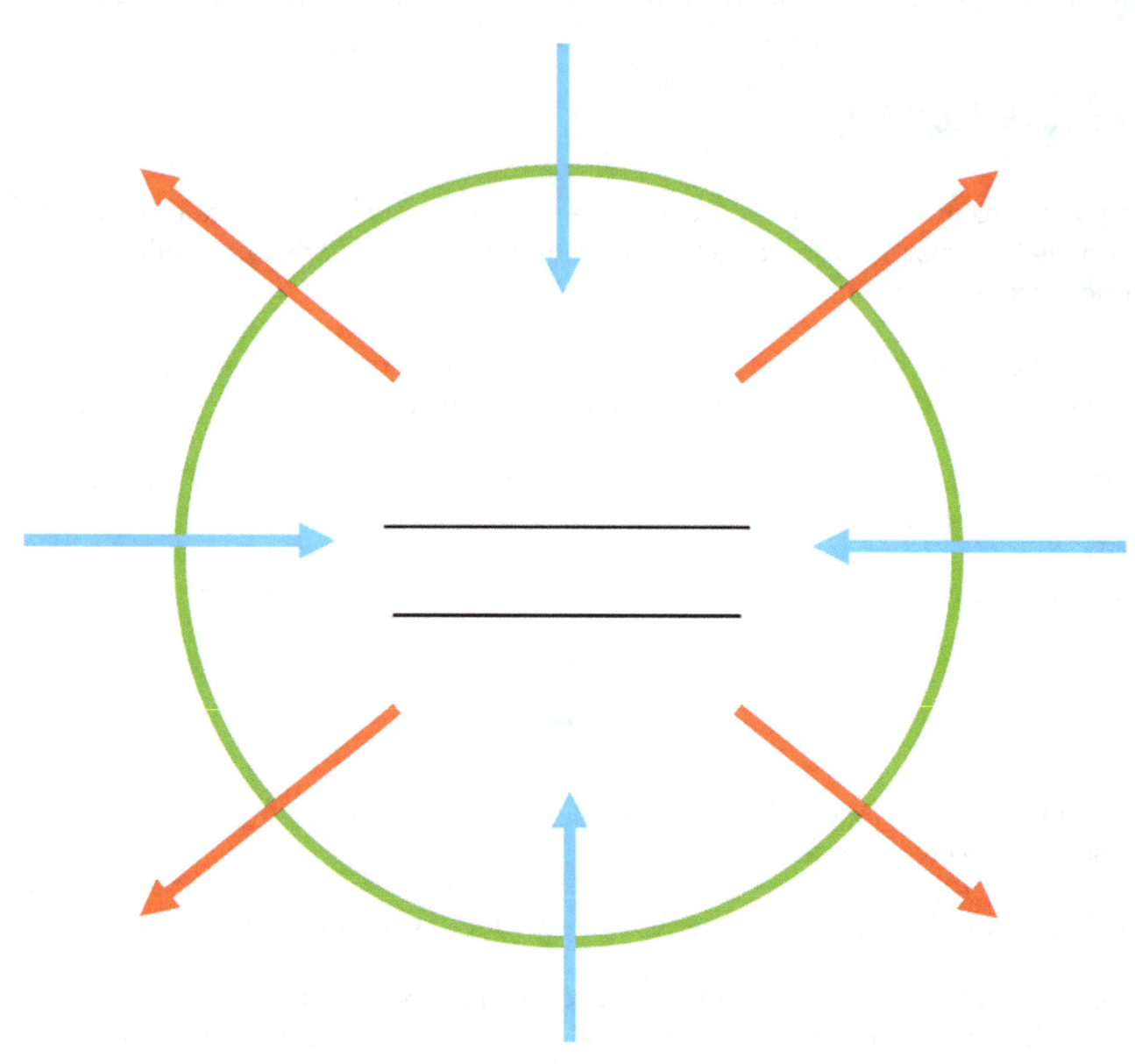

Reflect & Respond

1. Provide some examples of your grieving process when it comes to both giving up your out of control sexual behavior and recognizing the losses in your life that have been the result of your out of control sexual behavior.

    _____

    _____

    _____

2. Even though giving up the use of child sexual abuse media is healthy, what aspects of giving up the use of such media have you grieved?

    _____

    _____

    _____

3. On the circle illustration you completed above, which of your red arrows have been the greatest losses for you?

    _____

    _____

    _____

React #2

Take a blank sheet of paper and draw a piece of pottery that has been mended using Kintsugi. Use a gold or yellow marker to highlight the cracks in your pottery. Alongside the repaired cracks, write down useful tools for coping with grief, such as positive strategies you've learned (e.g., journaling, mindfulness, etc.) or the first name of a support person you can reach out to.

Porn Literacy

This exercise focuses on a somewhat controversial issue called "porn literacy." We believe that adult pornography can objectify individuals, create barriers to intimacy between sexual and romantic partners, and often exacerbate problematic sexual behaviors in those struggling with out-of-control sexual behavior. However, we also acknowledge that certain types of pornography can be incorporated into an individual's or couple's definition of healthy sexuality. Regardless of whether your pornography use is healthy or unhealthy, we recognize that many of you may continue to view adult pornography.

To state the obvious, we firmly believe it is never acceptable to view child sexual abuse media. This exercise is focused solely on the use of adult pornography.

We understand that the decision to stop using adult pornography may not be entirely your own. You may have probation restrictions that prohibit you from viewing it. The exercise will be helpful in understanding both your desire to use adult pornography and any "irritability" you may feel at having a restriction that prohibits its use.

If you choose to use adult pornography, we believe it should be an informed decision—one that is intentional and carefully considered. Understanding the definition of pornography, reviewing research on its effects, and weighing both the pros and cons of its use collectively form what we call "porn literacy."

In this exercise, we will break "porn literacy" down into five fundamental questions for you to answer. These questions will help you make a more informed decision regarding the use of adult pornography. We have included them as part of our standard Reflect & Respond section.

Reflect & Respond

1. What is pornography?

If you asked 100 people to define the word pornography, you would likely receive 100 different answers. People often struggle to define pornography and frequently use phrases like, "I'll know it when I see it," to avoid providing a concrete definition.

In reality, pornography can range from a single sexualized nude image or video to extremely disturbing content, including depictions of rape, torture, and even death. When you say to yourself, "I want to go online and look at porn," it is important to clearly define the type of pornography you intend to view.

So, what type of pornography do you intend to view? Do you believe the pornography you choose to watch is healthy for you—sexually, emotionally, and relationally?

_____

_____

_____

2. Do you know what the research says about pornography use?

Much of the research conducted by psychologists, therapists, and clinicians suggests that adult pornography use may not be entirely harmful for certain individuals. However, this research also highlights several variables that can make pornography use problematic. Four of the most concerning factors are discussed below:

a. High Sexual Disposition: This is a research term used to describe individuals with a high sex drive who struggle with out of control sexual fantasies, urges, and behaviors.

b. Hostile Masculinity: Men who exhibit hostile masculinity tend to be distrustful, insecure, and frequently angry. They often hold negative beliefs about both women and other men, particularly regarding gender roles and sexuality. These individuals believe it is their role to control others and assert dominance in all their relationships. They are highly sensitive to rejection and often blame others for their mistakes.

c. Impulsivity, Employment Problems, and Substance Use Issues: Any of these factors can indicate instability in a person's life, suggesting that their decision-making and problem-solving skills may be underdeveloped.

d. Hostile or Non-Supportive Peer Environment: Growing up in a hostile, dysfunctional, or non-supportive environment increases the likelihood of various struggles later in life. Research suggests that individuals from such backgrounds are more prone to problematic online sexual behaviors, including excessive adult pornography use or engaging in illegal sexual activity both online and offline.

Overall, research indicates that individuals with these characteristics are more likely to experience negative effects from pornography use. In fact, these factors may contribute to an escalation into more problematic behaviors, including the illegal use of child sexual abuse media.

Which of the characteristics noted in the research do you struggle with the most? Remember… **No Trained Seals!**

_____

_____

_____

3. Do you know why you want to view adult pornography?

While most people immediately associate adult pornography with sexual pleasure and satisfaction, many also use it as a "quick fix" or a way to escape reality.

Remember the Seven Desires? If not, go back and review them in Chapter 1, _Building the Foundations_, as pornography is often used by adults to fulfill one or more of these desires. It is quick, easy, and does not require a relationship with anyone other than yourself and a bit of digital content.

What are some reasons you think you want to look at adult pornography?

_____

_____

_____

4.   Do you understand the impact of your pornography use on others?

Many people believe their pornography use (along with related fantasies and masturbation) does not harm anyone. However, if you hope to develop a meaningful and intimate relationship with another person, your use of adult pornography will likely become an issue. Marriage and Family Therapists cite online sexual behaviors—such as pornography use and sexualized chatting—as one of the primary reasons couples seek therapy.

Even if you are not currently in a romantic or sexual relationship, pornography use can still interfere with the development of such a relationship. It can also impact your relationships with family members and friends. Your decision to use adult pornography should consider not only your own desires but also the potential impact on others.

Make a list of people who have already been affected by your pornography use, as well as those who could be harmed if you continue to view pornography.

_____

_____

_____

5.   Have you assessed the pros and cons of pornography use for your personal life?

Now that you have answered the four questions above, are you starting to understand that your decision to use adult pornography should not be taken lightly? We have often been told that this exercise "takes the fun out of watching porn." Sorry, not sorry. This is an important decision that requires careful consideration of the pros and cons. After all, you would not have purchased this book if you were not concerned about your decisions regarding your sexual behaviors.

Complete the Pros / Cons list below for viewing adult pornography:

Pros	Cons

React #1

We like iceberg metaphors. You might remember the iceberg from the "Building the Foundation" chapter. Now, we want you to take a look at the iceberg illustration below. Above sea level is your adult pornography use, but we encourage you to look below the surface before making your decision about whether or not to continue viewing adult pornography.

First, can you identify the feelings that arise when you want to view adult pornography? Are you sad, lonely, bored, or angry? Think about your past use of pornography and see if you can identify the emotions that may underlie your desire to engage with it. Are there other ways to cope with those emotions besides turning to adult pornography?

Next, consider the thoughts and beliefs you have about viewing adult pornography. What's the story you tell yourself? "It's no big deal." "I'm not harming anyone but myself." "No one will know." Can you say for certain that these thoughts are true, or are they just ways to rationalize your behavior and manage your emotions?

Finally, reflect on the Seven Desires again and determine what you are truly seeking when you use adult pornography. Is it closeness with others? Intimacy? Love?

Adult Porn Use

Feeling?
(Lonely, Angry, Sad, Anxious)

What is the story in my head about my porn use?
(I can escape, It will make me less anxious)

Consider which of the 7 Desires You Are Seeking
*(To be heard / To be understood
To be included / To be blessed / To be safe
To be chosen / To be affirmed)*

React #2

Now, you need to decide whether using adult pornography is a good choice in your life. It may be easy to convince yourself that the answer is yes, but this is not a decision you should make alone. You need to share your answers to each of the Reflect & Respond questions with multiple trusted individuals. This might include your therapist, support group, sponsor, accountability partner, probation officer, or a trusted friend or mentor. It is important to seek input from more than one person.

If you do not have a support system in place, you should postpone this decision until you have built one. Making this choice without external guidance increases the risk of falling into unhealthy patterns, including a potential relapse into viewing harmful content.

Notes

_____

_____

_____

_____

_____

_____

_____

_____

_____

Driving Your Own Self-Care Bus

Self-care is incredibly important to getting your out of control sexual behavior back under control. Taking care of yourself and living a healthy lifestyle makes it much easier to pull away from unhealthy behaviors. If you don't drive your own self-care bus, no one else will drive it for you!

In a similar vein, we all know that healthy eating, exercising, and getting enough sleep are important elements of feeling better about ourselves. However, in this exercise we will focus on four additional elements of self-care that you may not have considered before. These additional elements of self-care are journaling, considering medication, attending a 12-step group, and finding a therapist.

Journaling

Journaling gets a bad rap. It can often seem boring, and the act of writing about a mundane and ordinary life can sometimes feel as though it lacks creativity. However, we suggest that you expand your definition of what "journaling" can include. We like to think of journaling as everything from writing down your thoughts, to creating a piece of art that represents your feelings, to writing a poem or song. Journaling may even consist of doodles, collages, or mosaics. What we do know for sure is that taking down your thoughts and

feelings and getting them "outside of yourself" is always helpful and one of the easiest things you can do to begin taking care of yourself!

Consider Mental Health Medications

You may not think about mental health medications as a part of self-care. Both of us often see people who try everything we recommend, and yet they are still struggling with their out of control sexual behavior. This is because for some individuals, their out of control sexual behavior is also about their brain chemistry. While the exercises in this chapter will certainly be helpful, for some of you the exercises alone will not be enough for you to manage your out of control sexual behavior. Some of you may even realize that it is difficult to do the exercises at all, simply because you can't stop thinking about, or engaging in sexual behavior.

If this is true for you, set up an appointment with your primary care doctor, or even better, a psychiatrist who understands out of control sexual behavior. There are lots of medications that might be helpful to you. Medications that help with controlling out of control behaviors, or which address depression and anxiety are often prescribed to assist people with their out of control sexual behavior. Taking care of your brain is a great self-care activity!

Remember, it is *NOT* a weakness to use medications to assist in "zapping your cycle" and getting your out of control sexual behavior under control.

Imagine that a doctor has told you that you have diabetes, and there is medication that can help you! But you resist stubbornly because you think you can beat it on your own. Sure, diet and exercise can help, but diabetes is a diagnosis that will eventually *require* a medication intervention. You can try the exercises in this chapter and workbook, but like diabetics, you may need medication to address your out of control sexual behavior. Don't let your shame or ego stop you from getting better.

Something important to remember is that you can always make an appointment with a doctor and get information on possible medications. You may decide in this moment that you do not want to take medication, but once you have the information, you will always be able to make a different decision as needed further in the future.

Remember, "Knowledge = Power!"

Attend a 12-Step Group

Whether you consider your out of control sexual behavior an addiction or not, we are big believers in 12-Step S* groups (the S* stands for any sexual recovery group). Within these groups you can find community and support from people who understand the process of struggling with out of control sexual behavior. Plus these groups are FREE!

While there are online meetings available for you to attend, we suggest finding some in-person meetings that you can take part in. It is important to build an in-person support network and community. We understand that it is difficult to walk right into a meeting with strangers. In 12-Step S* meetings, you do not have to share any information. It is okay just to sit and listen to others, which is typically a very powerful experience for people who attend a 12-Step S* meeting.

It is also important to understand that while 12-Step S* groups take confidentiality seriously, it is safer to be cautious. We would not recommend sharing about your use of child sexual abuse media until you can develop some trust within your 12-Step S* Group. Most individuals in an S* group struggle with online pornography, and some will also struggle with child sexual abuse media. However, this issue may not be openly discussed in all 12-Step S* groups. Each meeting will have its own  personality. It may take trying a few different meetings to find one that feels safe and helpful for you.

There are at least five different large 12-Step S* groups that will be able to help you with your out of control sexual behavior. Below is a list of these groups, their webpages, and their phone numbers. In addition, we have listed a few prominent characteristics of each organization. Please note that not all of these groups operate in all geographic areas of the United States; however, some have meetings worldwide. All five of these

12-Step S* groups are free!

If you have trouble finding a sex-based 12-Step S* group in your area, find an online group or visit the Alcoholics Anonymous webpage and attend an AA meeting to get the support you need.

Sex Addicts Anonymous (SAA)

www.saa-recovery.org / (713) 869-4902
Flexible definitions of sexual health, including same-sex partners. Many meetings in the midwestern, eastern, and western parts of the U.S.

Sexaholics Anonymous (SA)

www.sa.org / (615) 370-6062
Strict definitions of sexual health, including no masturbation or sex outside of a male/female marriage. SA is the most Christian of the five groups. Likely the largest fellowship, with international attendance and many virtual and hybrid meetings.

Sex and Love Addicts Anonymous (SLAA)

www.slaafws.org / (210) 828-7900
Most flexible definition of sexual health across all five fellowships. Typically the meetings are co-ed. Sprinkled throughout the U.S. SLAA offers virtual/phone meetings.

Sexual Compulsives Anonymous (SCA)

www.sca-recovery.org / (800) 977-HEAL
Definition of sexual health includes same sex partners. Most popular in the Midwest U.S. and California.

Sexual Recovery Anonymous (SRA)

www.sexualrecovery.org / (607) 376-7721
Flexible definitions of sexual health, including same sex partners. Little information is available regarding this fellowship.

Find a Therapist

Many of you reading this workbook will already have a therapist, but if you do not, we recommend finding one. Everyone should have a therapist. We both have therapists, and they keep us sane… most of the time:)

Liam Marshall and his father, the late Bill Marshall, noted that therapists who have certain positive traits create the most effective therapeutic relationship with clients who have committed sexual offenses. These specific traits have been included in the word cloud below:

When seeking information about finding a therapist, you can also visit the organization Stop it Now (www.stopitnow.org). Click on the Help and Guidance Tab, then the Resource Library and the Finding and Choosing Professional Treatment link for more information on choosing a therapist.

You can visit the Stop it Now website or call Stop It Now (888-773-8368) for treatment referrals in your area.

Also, visit www.sash.net or www.iitap.com for referrals to therapists who are trained in treating out of control sexual behavior.

It is important to be sure any therapist you contact, including from these organizations, has training and expertise in treating sex offense behavior.

Reflect & Respond

1. Are there any of our four self-care suggestions that you find yourself resistant to trying? Why do you think that might be?

   _____

   _____

   _____

2. Can you think of other self-care activities that you would benefit from, but you seem resistant to do? What do you think that's about?

   _____

   _____

   _____

3. How do you think self-care (or lack of it) relates to your viewing of child sexual abuse media?

   _____

   _____

   _____

4. After reading this exercise, what do you plan to do differently regarding your self-care?

   _____

   _____

   _____

React

As you think about your own self-care and the four elements we mentioned above, if you were to choose any single one of those four to enact in your life, which would it be?

Can you plan and put into practice one of the self-care activities we suggested here? If not, is there another that you can bring into your own life?

Write down the specific details (including the when, where, what, how, and why) of your self-care plan.

Notes

_____

_____

_____

_____

_____

_____

_____

_____

_____

_____

ATTACK PLAN!!!

Before you begin, we are about halfway through the workbook. It's time to look back at the exercises you have completed, as well as the journal entries you have made. What things stood out to you as the most helpful? Which exercises gave you the best insights? What surprised you most? Make some notes about what you have learned so far, in particular what will be helpful in developing your plan of attack!

1/2

_____

_____

_____

_____

In this chapter you visited the doctor, became an electrician, and became porn literate! Wow! What a resumé! Now it's time to pull it all together and create a plan to finally address your out of control sexual behavior. That's what this exercise does, and hopefully the end result will be a plan you can hang on your wall. Ok… maybe not.

Time to ATTACK!!!

There is no Reflect & Response for this exercise. We want you to React and start building an ATTACK PLAN!!!

ATTACK PLAN!!!

Your Attack Plan!!! should be SMART (Specific, Measurable, Attainable, Relevant, and Time-bound). We want you to plan things you can do, not just think about doing. The following pages should help you create a plan that will help prevent out of control sexual behavior, as well as intervene if such behaviors begin to occur.

Meetings

☐ Identify 3-5 meetings that you could attend. At least one of these meetings should be in-person. The group may be a 12-Step S* Meeting (see resources provided earlier in this chapter) or another secular or religious group that addresses sexuality issues.

	Day/Time of Meeting	Address/Phone/URL	Contact Info
#1			
#2			
#3			

☐ Circle the number of the meeting you will attend first from the list above (make it as soon as possible) and list the date of that meeting you will attend.

#1   #2   #3   Date I will attend: _____

☐ I commit to attend _____ meetings in the next three months. Write the dates of the meetings you attended below.

_____   _____   _____   _____

_____   _____   _____   _____

_____   _____   _____   _____

_____   _____   _____   _____

Accountability

You should develop an accountability group of at least 5-10 people. Use these steps to help you.

☐ Write down the name and phone number or email of one person who can be your accountability partner. This should be someone from outside of your group and it should not be your significant other.

Name: _____

Contact Info: _____

☐ During your first week of group meetings, ask at least five people for their name and contact information. Record that information below.

Name: _____   Contact: _____

Name: _____   Contact: _____

Name: _____   Contact: _____

Name: _____   Contact: _____

Name: _____   Contact: _____

☐ During your first week of meetings, ask someone to serve as a temporary "sponsor" or accountability person. This will be someone from the group you are attending. If you are on probation, be sure to check with your probation officer to make sure they are ok with this step. List the person's name and contact information below.

Name: _____   Contact: _____

☐ Commit to making one contact per day for the next 30 days (at least half of these contacts should be phone calls - other contacts may be text messages, emails, etc.)

☐ Commit to contacting your sponsor or accountability person at least once per week over the next 30 days. This should be in addition to your daily contacts. List the four dates you will call your sponsor or accountability person:

_____ _____ _____ _____

Remember: You should call them more if necessary!

Abstinence

☐ Commit to an abstinence period of _____ days.

Journaling

☐ Purchase a nice journal and pen or find an app or piece of software that will encourage you to record your thoughts and feelings. Remember, journaling may not be just words, but can include phrases, poetry, song lyrics, pictures, and more.

☐ Make at least one journal entry (it could be just a single word!) for the next 90 days.

Counseling

☐ Do your research to locate a therapist that you think could be helpful. See our resources on this under the Self-Care exercise earlier in this chapter.

☐ Schedule a consultation session with a therapist and see how you "fit" with them. Don't feel bad if you want to try another therapist. Sometimes the chemistry just isn't there. Record your first appointment date below. If you already have a therapist, record your next session date below. You should be seeing your therapist at least twice a month. If not, step it up.

Appointment Date: _____

Self-Care

☐ Schedule a physical exam with your doctor (if you haven't had one in the last year). No doctor? Find one.

Doctor's Name: _____

Date of Exam: _____

☐ Get some exercise (walk the dog, hike, play pickleball, swim, etc.) Create a separate exercise log and record your activity for the next two weeks.

☐ Make healthier food choices and drink plenty of water. Create a separate food log and record all your food and water intake for the next two weeks.

☐ Get adequate sleep (7-8 hours per night). Record the number of hours of sleep for the next seven days.

_____   _____   _____   _____

_____   _____   _____

☐ Build community through leisure activities (e.g., hobbies, sports, spiritual and religious practices, meetup groups, etc.)

What will you focus on? _____

☐ Read at least one self-help book per month. What is the title of the first book on your list:

Title: _____

☐ Make a list of five positive affirmations about yourself to counteract your negative core beliefs. Examples: I am a courageous person for addressing my sexual issues. I am loved by others and by myself. My life has meaning and purpose.

_____

_____

_____

_____

_____

_____

_____

Medication Consultation

☐ If you suffer from depression, anxiety, ADHD, or other mental health issues OR you have tried repeatedly to stop your out of control sexual behavior without success, then you need to schedule an appointment with a psychiatrist. Research psychiatrists in your area by going online or asking friends and family for recommendations. Finding a psychiatrist who specializes in compulsive or addictive behavior is a bonus!

Doctor's Name: _____

Appointment Date: _____

Adult Pornography Use

☐ Based on the pornography literacy exercise earlier in this chapter, decide if you will continue to view adult pornography or steer clear of all pornography. Do not make this decision alone. Be sure to consult others about your rationale and decision.

I've decided to: _____

This was after consulting with: _____

Summary

This plan should help address your out of control sexual behavior, but it may need to be revisited on occasion. You will learn more about yourself and the plan may need to change as you develop a deeper understanding of who you are and the problems you face.

Sign below if you are committed to completing this ATTACK PLAN!!! By signing you are also agreeing to revisit this plan as necessary to update it and make any necessary revisions.

Finally, you are required to share this plan (even while it is in-progress) with at least one other person. Have them sign this plan to verify you reviewed it with them.

Initial Plan Signature:

_____   _____
Your Signature   Date

_____   _____
Accountability Partner Signature   Date

Updated Plan Signature:

_____   _____
Your Signature   Date

_____   _____
Accountability Partner Signature   Date

GREAT JOB!
MISSION ACCOMPLISHED!

Chapter 6: Technology Use

The focus of this chapter will be on helping you address your problematic technology use and on developing a plan to replace it with healthy technology use instead. Technology is here to stay, and we believe that even if you are currently restricted from using it, that doesn't have to mean that technology use is out of your reach forever. Safe and healthy technology use is possible for anybody!

Technology today is constantly changing, for example, AI is all the rage right now. We want to help you develop a plan so that no matter what technology appears in the future, you will be ready for it! It is important to be thoughtful and prepare yourself for using technology so you can keep yourself and others safe.

You know yourself best… you know what technologies you use, which ones cause you the most trouble, where you hide things, and how you keep secrets. This chapter will give you the basics, but you will need to apply them yourself for the exercises to be useful.

Let's Tech!

A List of Chapter Exercises

1. Technology Management
2. The Online Disinhibition Effect
3. The CyberHex
4. Technology Health Plan
5. Digital Footprints
6. Technology Craziness Index
7. Acceptable Use Plan

Don't Forget!

Those who have access to the Internet may want to visit our companion website for resources related to this and other chapters in the workbook. These resources include additional articles, websites, and copies of activities/graphics from the chapters.

http://www.internetbehavior.com/illegalimages

Notes

_____

_____

_____

_____

Technology Management

When we first started working in the field of online sexual offense behavior, there was only one device everyone had to worry about – the personal computer. Now there are cell phones (iOS and Droid), tablets, Kindles, computers, laptops, console gaming systems, portable gaming systems, Apple® Watches, etc., etc., etc.

The days of installing Net Nanny and feeling confident you won't ever see pornography again are long gone. This exercise will get you thinking about managing all your technology to the best of your ability – recognizing the software available isn't foolproof.

We are big believers in doing more than just installing software to manage your technology, however software is one tool that some people find useful when addressing their problematic online sexual behaviors and their involvement with child sexual abuse media.

Listed below are various software programs that may be helpful in reducing your exposure to child sexual abuse media. Software to assist with this can be categorized into two main areas: (1) blocking and filtering software and (2) monitoring/accountability software.

Blocking and Filtering Software

Blocking and filtering software is exactly what it sounds like: software designed to block and filter unwanted areas of the Internet. Blocking and filtering software can be installed on computers, cell phones, and other devices. Essentially, the software causes the device to preview the content of online information and media BEFORE it is actually displayed. If the content is deemed "inappropriate," the software stops it from being displayed on your computer, while content deemed "appropriate" by the software is let through to your display. Each software uses a different algorithm to determine "appropriate" content, but their goal is the same – to block and filter.

There are also "router" level (or DNS level) blocking and filtering programs. This just means that the blocking and filtering occurs before the content even reaches your device. This can be useful when managing a wi-fi network across an entire household. This way, any device in the house that connects to that wi-fi will automatically be filtered. This type of blocking and filtering works well but takes a little more tech skill to install and manage.

We hesitate to name any actual software packages here since they will probably be outdated by the time you read this workbook, but you can Google the term "Blocking and Filtering Software" to start getting some ideas.

Monitoring/Accountability Software

If blocking and filtering doesn't feel like enough for you, there is also monitoring/accountability software that "watches" you while you use your various technologies. It then sends a report to another person, someone who can review your activity and ask you about anything suspicious. This software is available for both computers and cell phones. Of course, this system relies on an accountability person (not a romantic partner or significant other!) who is willing to review the reports and confront you about any potential inappropriate behavior.

Again, we suggest Googling (when did that become a verb?) "Monitoring or Accountability Software" to get specific suggestions.

Notes

_____

_____

_____

_____

Reflect & Respond

1. Have you previously tried (or are you currently trying/ordered to use) any of these methods to manage your viewing of child sexual abuse media? If so, which methods did you find worked? Were there any that did not work for you? If you have not tried using any technology management programs, what are some reasons for your reluctance?

   _____

   _____

   _____

2. Which of the two types of software mentioned above do you think could be most helpful to you in reducing your risk of viewing child sexual abuse media? If you think neither would be helpful, why do you think that?

   _____

   _____

   _____

3. In total and complete honesty, have you ever tried to "work around" one of these software packages? By using a different device, logging on to a public wi-fi, guessing a password, etc.?

   _____

   _____

   _____

   _____

React

List one or two people that could be an accountability partner to you by "holding your password" or receiving reports about your technology use, should you decide to try these methods. Tell one of those individuals that you listed them as an accountability partner and see how they respond.

_____

_____

_____

If you are on probation, have an honest conversation with your probation officer about any attempts to "work around" their blocking, filtering or monitoring program. Also be sure to share with your probation officer the ways that blocking, filtering, or monitoring programs have been helpful in your attempts to change the way you use technology.

Notes

_____

_____

_____

_____

_____

_____

_____

The Online Disinhibition Effect

In 2004, Dr. John Suler, a professor at Rider University, wrote the following about the psychology of cyberspace:

"It's well known that people say and do things in cyberspace that they wouldn't ordinarily say or do in the face-to-face world. They loosen up, feel more uninhibited, and express themselves more openly. It's a double-edged sword. Sometimes people share very personal things about themselves. They reveal secret emotions, fears, and wishes, or they show unusual acts of kindness and generosity. On the other hand, the disinhibition effect may not be so benign, as individuals explore the dark underworld of the internet—places of pornography and violence—where they would never venture in the real world."

In his 2015 book, Psychology of the Digital Age: Humans Become Electric, Suler further described this phenomenon and named it the "Online Disinhibition Effect." He explained:

"What causes this online disinhibition? What is it about cyberspace that loosens psychological barriers? Several factors are at play. For some people, one or two of these factors produce the lion's share of the disinhibition effect. In most cases, though, these factors interact with and supplement each other, resulting in a more complex, amplified effect."

Elements of the Online Disinhibition Effect

1.   **You Don't Know Me** – This factor is driven by the anonymity the internet provides. When individuals feel anonymous, they are more inclined to engage in behaviors they would otherwise avoid. The anonymity of online environment fosters a sense of detachment from real-world consequences.

2. **You Can't See Me** – Although related to anonymity, this refers to the sense of invisibility many internet users experience. Feeling invisible and unseen leads individuals to believe they can neither cause nor suffer consequences for their online behavior. The opportunity to be physically invisible amplifies the disinhibition effect.

3. **See You Later** – This concept revolves around the illusion that one can simply "escape" negative online behaviors (e.g., trolling, cyberbullying, viewing pornography) by deleting a message, closing a browser, or logging off. The perceived ease of disengagement makes it easier to engage in risky behavior in the first place.

4. **It's All in My Head** – The boundary between reality and fantasy often blurs in the online world. This "fantasy world" encourages actions and speech that individuals would likely avoid in the offline world. Some justify viewing harmful content as "just a fantasy."

5. **It's Just a Game** – Many perceive the virtual world as a game where real-world rules and norms do not apply. Once they log off, they assume their online actions have no real impact. This mindset leads some to believe they are not accountable for their digital behavior.

6. **We're Equals** – The internet creates the illusion of a level playing field where age, gender, wealth, and race become irrelevant. While this can foster positive interactions, it also facilitates inappropriate relationships, including those between adults and minors. An older man might never approach a group of teenagers in a mall, but online, where everyone seems equal, such interactions feel less unnatural, making it easier for harmful behaviors to occur.

Reflect & Respond

1. Do you feel like the Online Disinhibition Effect played a role in your viewing of child sexual abuse media? How?

   _____

   _____

   _____

2. If you said yes to #1, which of the specific elements of the Online Disinhibition Effect most influenced your online sexual behavior, and more specifically your viewing of online child sexual abuse media?

   _____

   _____

   _____

3. What percentage of your online sexual offense behavior would you attribute to the Online Disinhibition Effect?

   _____

   _____

   _____

4. What is your plan for creating more awareness of Online Disinhibition Effect when you are using technology? We have provided one creative activity below that will help in this process but think of other specific things you can do. You may need to ask your support community for help on this one.

   _____

   _____

   _____

React

Take each of the elements of Suler's Online Disinhibition Effect and create a collage, picture, song, rap, poem, etc. You may want to feature the elements that are most relevant to your problematic online sexual behavior. There is no "right way" to do this project. The only requirement is that you pair the words you use with some type of imagery, picture, songs, etc and that your project is meaningful to you.

We believe this project will help your brain more easily recall the elements of the Online Disinhibition Effect when you are using technology.

Notes

_____

_____

_____

_____

_____

_____

_____

_____

_____

The CyberHex

In addition to the Online Disinhibition Effect described in the previous exercise, there is another similar concept known as the "CyberHex." The CyberHex is a six-sided figure (hexagon, get it?) where each side represents a different facet of technology. When these features combine, they create a "hex," or trance-like state. The synergy created through the interaction of the CyberHex factors makes current day technology more seductive to its users than any of its predecessors (e.g., television, radio, etc.).

CyberHex Concepts and Definitions *Integral, Imposing, Inexpensive, Isolating, Interactive, Intoxicating*	
Integral	Technology has become such an integral part of our lives; it has become impossible to avoid. Even if an individual decided never to use technology again and to go "off-grid," the ways that technology is integrated into both our society and culture would make that nearly impossible. Most people need technology for work, banking, doctors' appointments, communicating with others, etc. As you can imagine, this integration has both positive and negative aspects. For individuals struggling with child sexual abuse media, it means they have to develop strategies for using technology in healthy ways.
Imposing	The amount of general information that can be found through technology is staggering. This is true of sexual material as well. Technology provides an endless supply of sexual material 24 hours a day, 7 days a week, and 365 days a year. Such a significant amount of child sexual abuse media can facilitate incorrect beliefs like, "Everyone does this," "It is normal," "No one is being harmed," and "There are no consequences."

CyberHex Concepts and Definitions
Integral, Imposing, Inexpensive, Isolating, Interactive, Intoxicating

Inexpensive	For a relatively small fee, or often for no fee at all, one can access an immense amount of online media (both sexual and non-sexual) using technology. In the offline world, such excursions can be extremely expensive and cost prohibitive. Technology overrides that cost prohibition and makes it easy to access a staggering amount of information and media, including child sexual abuse media. he word "free" implies "at no cost." In the online world, it is easy to assume that "free" also implies, "There is nothing wrong with using child sexual abuse media, it's free," or that, "There must not be any consequences if it is free."
Isolating	Technology can be isolating. Even though interpersonal relationships may develop between people through technology, these relationships often do not require the same level of emotional investment that offline relationships require. The isolation and anonymity provided by technology can be a welcome relief from "real peopling" all day. Everyone needs short breaks from others in the offline world; however, sometimes the isolation of the online world stops being a short break and becomes a person's "drug of choice," which they consistently use to avoid, anesthetize, and escape from the demand of offline relationships and "real" life.
Interactive	While technology is isolating it also "hooks" individuals into forming online "relationships" – some of which are healthy, and some of which are usually not. These "relationships" can approximate reality, but they are not real relationships. They do not involve the give and take of an offline relationship, and they do not involve the same skills necessary for developing healthy, emotionally intimate relationships. Most importantly, the online world facilitates the collapse of boundaries between individuals, making everyone seem like an equal. When this online equality is misused or misapplied, it can encourage sexual conversations and sexual fantasies that would never occur in the offline world.

CyberHex Concepts and Definitions
Integral, Imposing, Inexpensive, Isolating, Interactive, Intoxicating

Intoxicating	This intoxication is the phenomenon that occurs when you combine the first five elements of the CyberHex. This combination makes for an incredibly intoxicating element that is often difficult to resist. This pleasure is most likely from a chemical released in the brain that you begin to crave and return to over and over again. Just like anything that brings us pleasure – we want more of it! And of course, when sexual arousal is involved, it makes the intoxicating effect of the CyberHex even more powerful.

The combination of these factors often creates an "autopilot bubble" where individuals start viewing, scrolling, listening, etc. without much connection to the real world. Remember when you start checking your email or social media "one last time" before bed and before you know it, three hours have passed. That's because of the CyberHex – the trance-like state technology induces. This same effect can occur when viewing pornography online – hours pass, images increase in intensity, the ages in the images/videos get younger, etc. Rarely does anyone use mindfulness when using technology. That is why those mindfulness skills from Chapter Two are so important!

When the CyberHex and the Online Disinhibition Effect (discussed in the previous exercise) are paired with the lure and reinforcement of sexual arousal, technology becomes the "ideal" environment for problematic online sexual behavior, including the viewing of child sexual abuse media.

Reflect & Respond

Review each of the six dimensions of the CyberHex above. Consider each one carefully as they relate to your viewing of child sexual abuse media. On the illustration of the CyberHex, you will notice there is a line that looks like this: _____%. Place a number into each cell of the CyberHex to indicate the estimated percentage that each particular factor played in YOUR viewing of child sexual abuse media.

For example, if you believe that "Isolation" is the biggest factor leading to your viewing of child sexual abuse media, you may want to assign that factor 50% or more. Some cells may have a zero in them, while others may be close to 100%. This process will involve some honest reflection on your part. At the end, be sure all the numbers total 100%.

By placing these percentages on the CyberHex, you will have a clearer picture of what aspects of technology contributed to your use of child sexual abuse media. While there are multiple reasons for engaging in such behavior, this exercise will help you to more clearly identify which areas of the CyberHex contributed significantly to your behavior.

The CyberHex

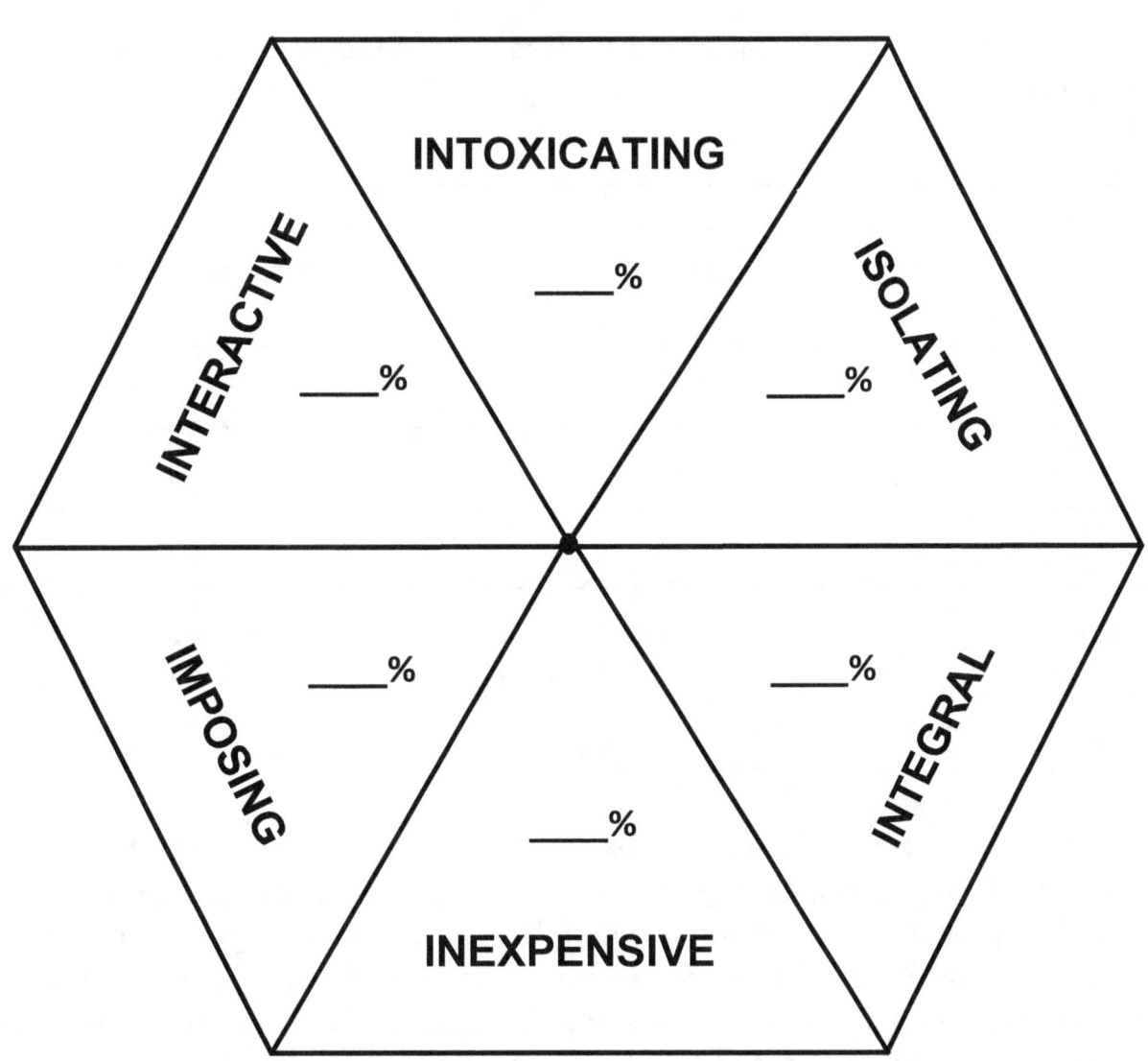

React #1

Now that you have a better understanding of which aspects of the CyberHex contributed to your viewing of child sexual abuse media, it's time to develop some management techniques to help you cope with those elements of the CyberHex.

List below some things you can do to prevent CyberHex elements from occurring or what you will do when they "sneak up" on you. Place the CyberHex elements you are addressing in parentheses next to the action you will take.

Example: Only use technology when others are around (isolation)

Example: Take at least 12 consecutive hours off of all technology 1x/week (imposing)

_____

_____

_____

_____

_____

_____

React #2

Share your insights and this CyberHex exercise with your therapist, group, probation officer, accountability partner, sponsor, or other trusted individuals. This will help ensure you are seeing the full picture. It is not a good idea to use your partner/significant other as your trusted individual, as this sets up a problematic dynamic in the relationship. You may decide to share this exercise with your partner/significant other but do so with the help of your therapist.

Digital Footprints

Digital Footprints refer to the trails and traces we leave behind as we navigate the world of technology. Just like in the real world, when we "step" somewhere, we leave a mark of where we have been. In the digital world, there is no instant visual mark left behind, so it is easy to forget that digital footprints are being created.

The Online Disinhibition Effect and the "Cyberhex" can influence the decisions we make in the online environment, the behaviors we engage in online, and ultimately, our digital footprint. Research has shown that when we experience the elements of these phenomena, we are more likely to take risks and engage in inappropriate and often illegal online behaviors.

Monitoring your digital footprint moving forward will be an important step in your overall technological health. Complete the following exercise to help you better understand your digital footprint.

1. Using the pair of footprints below, write your name on both footprints. This signifies that **you** are taking responsibility for your digital footprint and are accountable for wherever you "walked" in the past while using technology and wherever you "walk" in the future.

2. Place the name of a trusted friend, family member, sponsor, etc., who knows about your current problem with your online sexual behavior in the footprint on the right. This person will be your accountability partner for your digital footprint. If you have more than one individual who can function as an accountability partner in this regard, add their names to the footprint on the right as well. When you step into a negative or unhealthy area online, this should be the person in whom you confide your misstep. They will also be someone who can help you prevent online problems by asking about your digital behavior and someone you can confide in about any lapses or relapses you experience while using technology.

3. You are going to color in the two big toes on the footprints. On the left toe, scribble outside the lines (pretend you are in preschool). Color the big toe on the right, carefully staying within the lines. This represents the difference between going outside the boundaries online versus honoring the boundaries to stay safe and healthy online.

4. On the left footprint, which has the scribbled-out toe, list the boundaries that you have crossed in the past when using technology. On the right footprint, which has the neatly colored toe, list the boundaries you think will be important to maintain when you use technology in the future. These may be your own personal boundaries or the boundaries of others. Honoring boundaries shows respect for yourself and others in the digital world.

5. Using a marker, write the words "child sexual abuse media" on the left footprint. As you have made the decision to begin working through this workbook, you have decided you want to erase those words. Go ahead… try to erase or scribble them out.

Pay attention to the fact that no matter how hard you try, there are still remnants of those words. This is to remind you that whatever you do online is stored somewhere and cannot be erased. There is no such thing as deleting your digital footprint or your behaviors when using technology—so make your choices wisely.

6. On the left footprint, list various activities and behaviors you engaged in in the past that did not support a healthy digital footprint. On the right footprint, list various activities and behaviors you could engage in while using technology that would support a healthy and safe digital footprint (e.g., listen to music, listen to appropriate podcasts, watch a TED Talk, communicate with others who support you, go online only when others are around, etc.).

7. The best way to manage your digital footprint is to work on developing a positive reputation for yourself while using technology. You can do this by making healthy choices, staying in "safe" zones (your green zone from the Technology Health Plan Exercise), following your boundaries, and not provoking others. Write a few words or phrases on your right footprint that describe who you want to be in the digital world. Use the tools provided in this chapter to work towards building that reputation through your online decisions and behaviors.

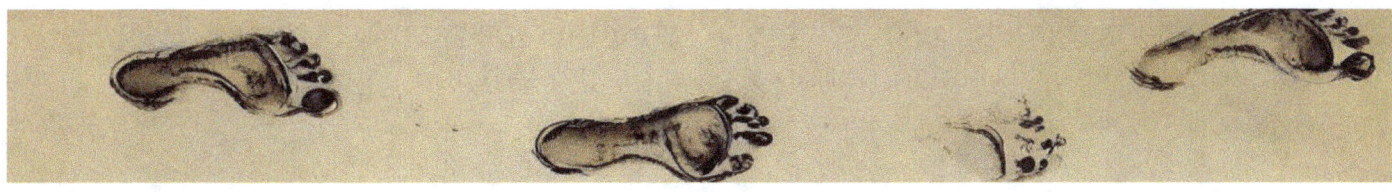

Reflect & Respond

1. What did your past digital footprint say about you?

_____

_____

_____

2. What does your current digital footprint say about you?

_____

_____

_____

3. What do you hope your future digital footprint will say about you?

_____

_____

_____

_____

_____

_____

_____

4. Do you think it would be difficult to tell your therapist and/or accountability person that your digital footprint is in jeopardy? Why or why not?

    _____

    _____

    _____

5. What is your plan for keeping a positive digital footprint in the future?

    _____

    _____

    _____

React

Share your digital footprint with another human being (no dogs allowed!). This could be a close friend, group member, therapist, probation officer, or other trusted adult. You can share your digital footprint with more than one person.

We would not encourage sharing the footprint with your significant other. They may feel responsible for helping you maintain your footprint and that is not their job!

Notes

_____

_____

_____

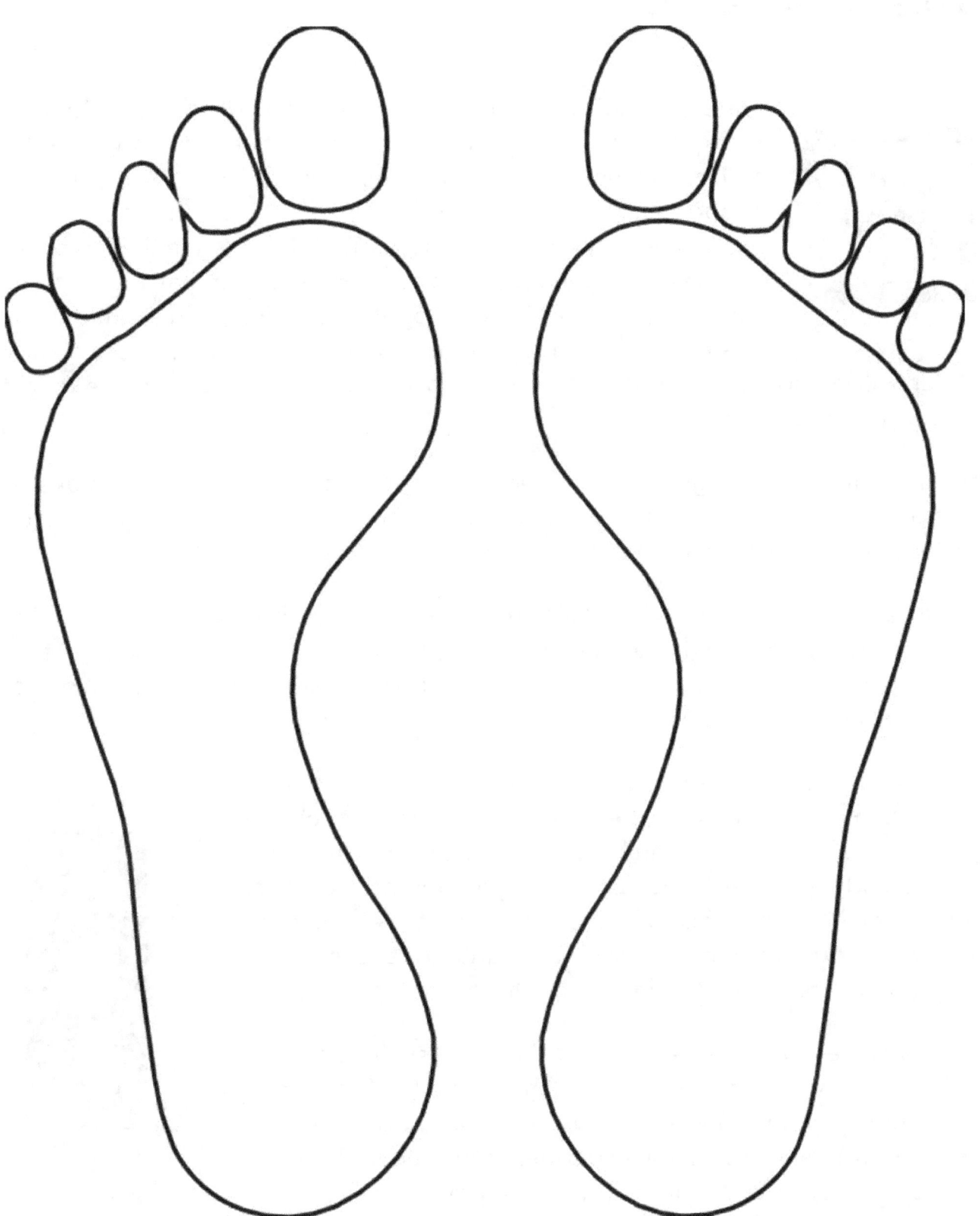

Technology Health Plan

The circle plan is a Technology Health Plan divided into four sections representing different aspects of healthy and unhealthy technology use. Those four sections are: (1) Emotions, (2) Thoughts, (3) Behaviors, and (4) Situations. The purpose of this exercise is to help you develop a Technology Health Plan of your own. As you develop your plan, it is important that you recognize which of your emotions, thoughts, behaviors, and situations related to technology are unhealthy and which ones are healthy. This plan will change and evolve as you learn more about yourself and master effective technology management skills.

There is a blank Technology Health Plan at the end of this exercise. You can make copies of the blank one for future use or can print blank copies from the companion website: www.internetbehavior.com/illegalimages.

In the inner circle, or the "red zone," list emotions, thoughts, behaviors, and situations related to technology use that are **never** healthy for you. These unhealthy aspects of technology use may include items such as using technology after 10:00 p.m., or viewing child sexual abuse media, etc.

The middle circle is the "yellow zone." In the yellow zone, you should list emotions, thoughts, behaviors, and situations related to your technology use that can be a "slippery slope." The yellow zone can lead you towards the red zone if you do not intervene. Examples include using the computer when you are alone, going online when you are hungry, angry, lonely, tired, or stressed (HALTS), or for some people viewing adult pornography, etc.

The outer circle is your "green zone." This circle lists thoughts, emotions, behaviors, and situations related to **healthy** technology use. Examples might include attending an online support meeting, connecting with an accountability partner, using technology alongside responsible individuals or at safe times, visiting healthy, appropriate areas online, etc.

A sample Technology Health Plan has been provided to help you understand how to complete your own Technology Health Plan. To Reflect & Respond in the next section, you need to fill in the zones of your Technology Health Plan. Use the example provided on the next page to help get you started.

Reflect & Respond

1. Which zone of the Technology Health Plan did you find most difficult to complete? What made it difficult for you?

    _____

    _____

    _____

2. How does the number of items listed in your green zone compare to the number listed in your yellow and red zones? What do you think the differences mean?

    _____

    _____

    _____

3. What is the estimated percentage of time you spend in each zone? Do you feel like you need to make a shift in this percentage, or are you happy with it?

    _____

    _____

    _____

4. Develop some strategies you can use when you enter the yellow or red zones. Maybe you call your accountability person or your therapist? Maybe you have a rule that you immediately shut down your device and got for a walk or take a moment to breathe. It is important that you come up with strategies that make sense for you!

    _____

    _____

    _____

5. Your plan may be most effective if you share it with someone else. Would you consider sharing it with another person (e.g., support network, therapist, group, etc.)? Why or why not?

_____

_____

_____

React

Get out your daily planner, calendar, journal, etc. and make a note for six weeks from today. This is when you will revisit your Technology Health Plan.

When you revisit the plan, pay attention to what is working and what is not. Remember you need to make copies of the blank Technology Health Plan at the end of this exercise or print bank copies from the companion website.

When revisiting your Technology Health Plan, consider the following questions. Can you add any emotions, thoughts, behaviors, or situations related to technology use to the green zone, which you've learned are safe? Conversely, how are things going in the red zone? Is there anything you need to add to the red zone? Has anything in the yellow zone moved to red?

If you don't have access to technology because of court-related restrictions, don't worry. Create your plan now and then consult it when you have access again. Be sure to do the six-week update after you resume using technology.

We want you to regularly return to your Technology Health Plan so that you are always reflecting on what is working and how it may need to be revised and updated.

Notes

_____

_____

_____

_____

_____

_____

_____

_____

_____

_____

_____

_____

_____

_____

_____

Technology Health Plan

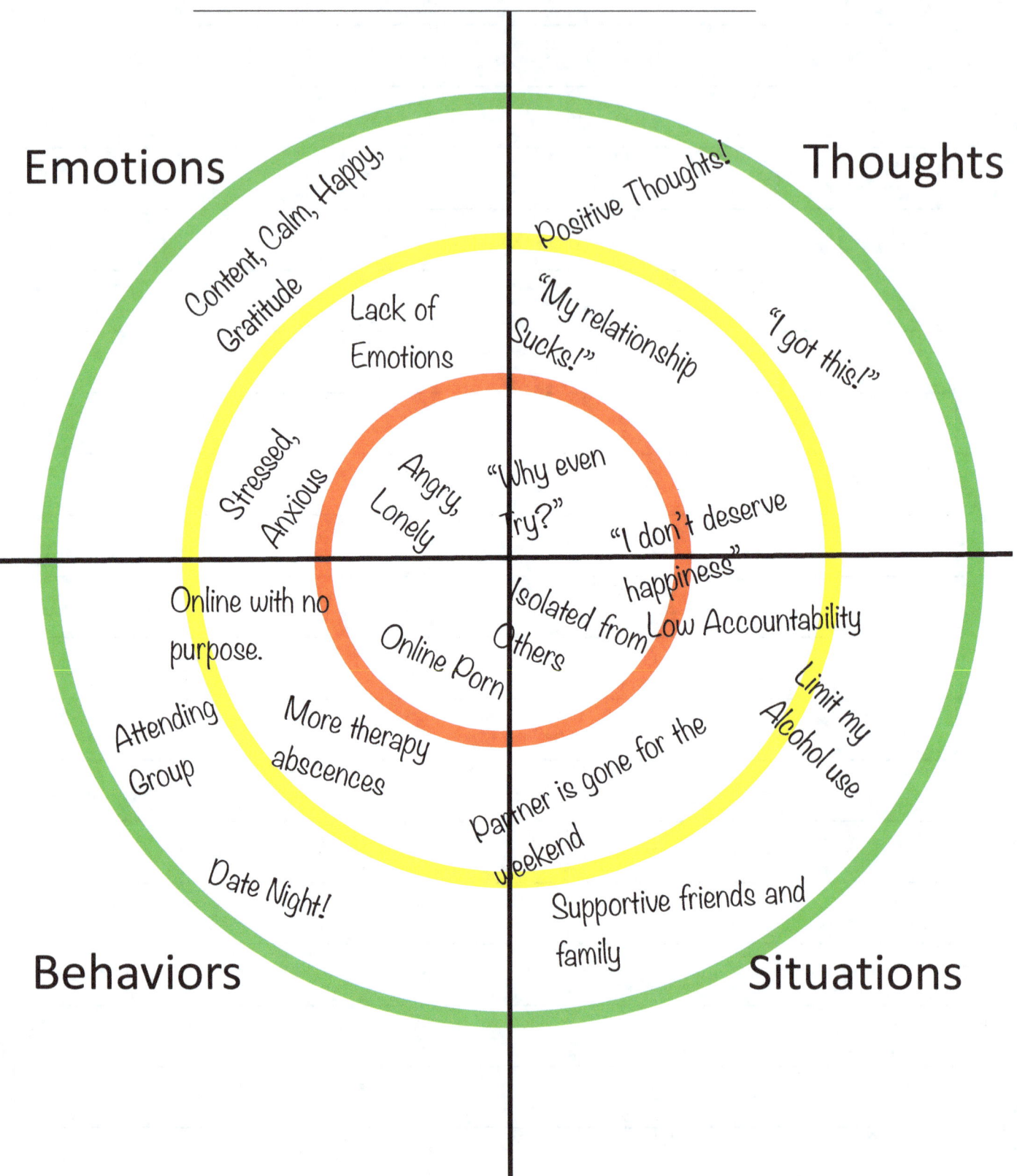

Emotions

Thoughts

Content, Calm, Happy, Gratitude

Lack of Emotions

Positive Thoughts!

"My relationship Sucks!"

"I got this!"

Stressed, Anxious

Angry, Lonely

"Why even Try?"

"I don't deserve happiness"

Online with no purpose.

Online Porn

Isolated from Others

Low Accountability

Attending Group

More therapy abscences

Partner is gone for the weekend

Limit my Alcohol use

Date Night!

Supportive friends and family

Behaviors

Situations

Technology Health Plan

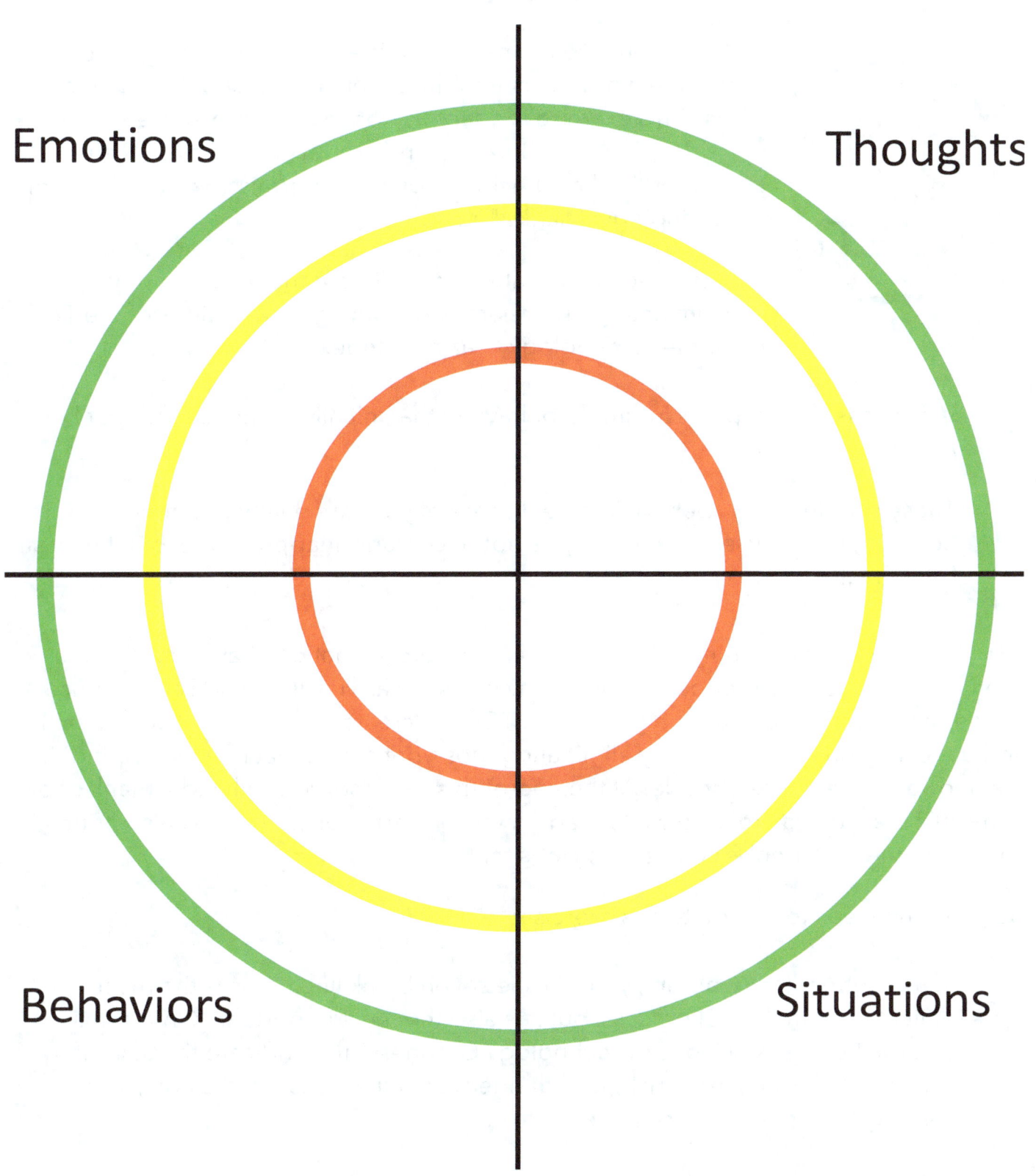

Emotions

Thoughts

Behaviors

Situations

Technology Craziness Index

Don't you love the name of this exercise? Anything that has the word "craziness" in it seems like it should apply to us! This exercise is adapted from a similar exercise known as the "Personal Craziness Index" developed by Dr. Patrick Carnes. He has graciously given us permission to adapt it for technology. Thanks Pat!

The concept is relatively simple, but the results can be illuminating. There are two working assumptions of the TCI, or the "Technology Craziness Index"…

1. "Craziness" first appears in simple behaviors that initially do not seem "that bad." And…

2. These simple "crazy" behaviors reveal some of your unhealthy patterns. Sometimes your use of technology is not necessarily inappropriate, but it may still be unhealthy.

The TCI can help you identify the buildup of minor problematic behaviors which may eventually lead to more serious online behaviors, such as viewing child sexual abuse media. When used correctly, the goal of the TCI is to create a balance between healthy and unhealthy online behavior by eliminating those behaviors that may be tipping the scale towards the unhealthy side. At the end of this exercise, you will find a blank copy of the TCI that you can refer to while reading these instructions. You may also print a copy from the workbook's companion website.

Here are the steps to complete this exercise:

1. In the bottom left quadrant, you will see seven blank lines. This is the most difficult step in the TCI process, but it is also the most important. On these lines you will list the "Key Signs of Technology Craziness" that indicate the start of a "build-up" towards more risky and dangerous online sexual behaviors, such as viewing child sexual abuse media.

The trick here is that you are looking for small signs that are likely to indicate the start of a growing problem. Many of these things may not even seem like a problem on their own, but over time they can build up. For example, if pouring a glass of wine or grabbing a beer before you sit down to mindlessly scroll on your phone leads to viewing pornography, you would want to list "pouring a glass of wine" on one of the lines as an example of a key sign. Bulleted below are some other examples of "key signs" of technology craziness. Please note, these may, or may not be our personal examples 😊 You may want to take a week or so to observe your routines, rituals, and behaviors before completing this exercise.

- Ignoring others due to my technology use.
- Texting while driving.
- Using technology "after hours".
- Quickly checking email turns into a multi-hour event.
- Amazon window shopping.
- Interacting with random strangers online.
- Mindlessly eating / drinking while using technology.

2. The top half of the TCI is for tracking your seven key signs each day over a six-week period. This should give you enough data to identify patterns that may emerge.

Each week is represented by a single column. Each column has a place for all seven days. In the appropriate "cell" you will indicate how many of your chosen key signs occurred on that single day. Don't be concerned with which ones occurred when, it is simply a count of how many times a key sign occurred in a day. A key sign may occur multiple times in a single day – if so, count it multiple times.

If you forgot to take the time to complete the TCI then you get a "7" for the day!

At the end of the week, you will enter a total for the week at the bottom of the column. Use the bottom right quadrant to interpret your score and enter it into the appropriate box under the total.

During and following the completion of the TCI, consider the following questions.

Reflect & Respond

Examine the data you collected for the following patterns. Begin by circling any number that is 5 or higher.

1. Look at each day (Sunday to Saturday) in Week #1, in Week #2, etc. When there were high numbers within an individual week, see if you can recall what was happening on that particular day? Were you struggling with something? Stressed out? Anxious? Angry? Tired? Something else? Jot down some notes below explaining what you remember about those particular troublesome days.

    _____

    _____

    _____

2. Look <u>across</u> the weeks for recurring high numbers. Are there certain days of the week that always seem to be high? Saturdays for example? Ask yourself about those days of the week. What happens on those high number days? Are you home? Bored? Lonely? Rushed doing errands? Feeling entitled after a long week? Jot down some notes about any patterns you notice emerging on the same day of the week across the entire TCI.

    _____

    _____

    _____

3. Finally, take a look at the totals across the week. How did you do? Was there consistency? Was it mostly high? Mostly low? Varied? If it varied, do you know why? Can you guess what was happening on high weeks or low weeks?

    _____

    _____

    _____

4. If you were to complete a Technology Craziness Index again, would you choose the same seven key indicators? If not, what else would you choose? How do you think changing the key indicators would have changed the data you collected?

_____

_____

_____

React

Hopefully, this exercise highlighted how the "small things matter." While the "big" behaviors may have more consequences, there are individual steps that precede them that can be avoided to help you avoid the big online mistakes.

After reflecting on your patterns, create a list of things you can do to address these patterns. If Saturdays are always "high" days, what needs to change on Saturdays? If one week was a great score, what can you learn from this to apply to other weeks?

Write some thoughts about your plan to keep yourself from going "crazy."

_____

_____

_____

_____

_____

_____

Technology Craziness Index (TCI) Tracking Sheet   Name::

	Week 1	Week 2	Week 3	Week 4	Week 5	Week 6
Sunday						
Monday						
Tuesday						
Wednesday						
Thursday						
Friday						
Saturday						
Weekly PCI Total						
Interpretation of the number						

My 7 Key Signs of Technology Craziness (Build-up Warning Signs)

1. _____
2. _____
3. _____
4. _____
5. _____
6. _____
7. _____

Interpretation of the PCI numbers

If the numbers are from **0-9**, that means you are **Healthy**

If the numbers are from **10-19**, that means you are **Stable**

If the numbers are from **20-29**, that means you are **On the Edge**

If the numbers are from **30-39**, that means you are **Falling**

If the numbers are from **40-49**, that means you are **Over the Edge**

Acceptable Use Plan (AUP)

We have a love-hate relationship with rules. After all, we need them to know what we can and can't do, but we also hate being told what to do. We have to remind ourselves that rules are about safety. Have you ever read the directions on certain products? *"Don't use this hair dryer while showering."* Ok, who needed that rule? Well, someone did, and we'd hate to think of what happened to the person who didn't know this rule and showered while drying their hair! Zzzzap!

The goal of creating an Acceptable Use Plan (AUP) is to help you establish a set of rules for your technology use. These rules will not be set by someone else, but will instead be created by you, for you. This is because nobody knows more about the specifics of your technology use than you do. It wouldn't do any good for us to create a set of rules for you that may not have any relevance to your own personal online situation. For example, we could make a rule that says, "Don't use technology after 9:00 p.m." But if you work a second shift job that keeps you away from technology in the evenings anyway, then that rule won't be helpful for you. Instead, we are going to ask you to reflect on your situation and your technology use and then to set a list of parameters (rules) that will help keep you (and others) safe online.

There are 10 main areas we want you to consider when establishing your Acceptable Use Plan. These are named and defined below:

Acceptable Use Plan (AUP) Directions

Section Name	Definition
Preamble	Use this section to remind yourself why you need an Acceptable Use Plan, how it will keep you safe online, and how it will help you stop viewing child sexual abuse media.
Time and Place	Many people who struggle with viewing child sexual abuse media have certain times and places where using their computer/phone/tablet is more dangerous for them. For example, some can't access the Internet after 10:00 p.m., since that's when their defenses are down, and they will get into trouble. Others have no trouble using technology at work but using it in the attic or basement of their home is triggering. Use this section to define where and when technology use is acceptable and not acceptable for you.
Meeting Others	Meeting others online is a common occurrence, but the online world has created some problems for you. Meeting others both online and offline should have very specific parameters. This is the section to outline who you can talk to online and who you can't. Also, make a list of which online contacts it is ok for you to meet in the offline world, and which are not. Be specific and clear. For example, meeting someone from your online support group may be good to meet face to face, but meeting a past sex-chat partner is not a good idea.
Respectful Communication	Research has shown that those who troll or bully others online also tend to "act out" sexually while online as well. Define what respectful online communication looks like to you, and then follow your own guidelines to avoid being an ass online.

Section Name	Definition
Blocking / Filtering / Monitoring	We have discussed online software for blocking, filtering, and monitoring digital devices. If you choose to use these methods, this section should define any rules related to them (e.g., I will not attempt to work around the filters; I will tell my accountability partner if it seems the software is not working correctly, etc.). Also, establish a clear accountability partner that is not your significant other, and list their name here. Have a plan to reach out to them about any "glitches" in your software.
Usernames and Passwords	You should use this section to list all your usernames and passwords (including gamertags and other online identities) across all the sites you access, especially social media sites. Also, if you have any sexualized usernames or passwords – change them. You are more likely to get in trouble if your username is @bighungdaddy. Also, make a separate list of your usernames and passwords and share them with your accountability partner.
Unacceptable Activities	Remember the Technology Health Plan with the red, green, and yellow circles? Go look at that again and see what you have in the red and yellow circles. Those are likely the things you will list here. This section should include the "Hard NO!" activities and a couple of "Probably NO!" items.
What to do if?	It is important to consider what you will do if something goes wrong and you violate this document. Think about what you will do if a "pop-up" window appears on your screen with sexual images, or if you happen to run across an inappropriate post, or if you end up being an ass to someone else online. Be specific about what you will do and who you will tell if this happens.
Consequences	What will happen if you violate your plan? Will you agree to take a break from technology? Will you revise your plan? Will you tell someone about your online choices/behaviors? Be clear about the consequences you will give yourself.

Section Name	Definition
Conclusions	Think about the spirit of this plan. You won't be able to list everything you can and cannot do, so you may need to reckon with other behaviors "on the fly" further down the line. Just because a behavior is not specifically listed here doesn't mean it's ok. Remember, this plan is not here to punish you; it is here to protect you.

Remember, the AUP is here to help you establish a set of rules and boundaries for yourself. While working on your AUP, we want you to remember the "Trained Seal" exercise from the "Building the Foundation" Chapter of this workbook. A Trained Seal will approach their AUP in order to please others. They will set the rules that they think others want them to set. Don't do this! Don't be a Trained Seal while working on your AUP - practice rigorous honesty instead. Taking the honest approach will be the best way to prevent any future viewing of child sexual abuse media.

Reflect & Respond

1. Individuals who struggle with viewing child sexual abuse media often admit they have issues with rules and boundaries. How do you feel about rules and boundaries? How does your attitude about rules and boundaries influence your attitude about this exercise?

_____

_____

_____

2. Have you tried setting limits or rules about your technology use before? Did it work? Why or why not? How can you make this time a success?

_____

_____

_____

3. What is your #1 Top Rule that you MUST follow for yourself in order to prevent your viewing of child sexual abuse media in the future?

_____

_____

_____

React

A blank Acceptable Use Plan is provided on the next page (you may want to make extra copies before writing on it). Use the information provided above to create your first draft of an AUP for yourself. Feel free to create your AUP in a different format If our format does not work for you. Just make sure to include all the various areas of the AUP that we have discussed.

Keep in mind, you will likely need to return to this AUP to make changes and revisions as you learn more about yourself throughout this workbook. There will also be a copy of the blank Acceptable Use Plan on the companion website: www.internetbehavior.com/illegalimages. And remember, **NO TRAINED SEALS!**

Notes

_____

_____

_____

_____

_____

_____

Acceptable Use Plan (AUP) Template

Section Name	Your Rules
Preamble	
Time and Place	
Meeting Others	
Respectful Communication	

Section Name	Your Rules
Blocking / Filtering / Monitoring	
Usernames / Passwords	
Unacceptable Activities	
What to do if?	

Section Name	Your Rules
Consequences	
Conclusions	

Signature:

_____   _____
Your Signature   Date

_____   _____
Accountability Partner Signature   Date

Chapter 7: Victim Awareness

If you have ever viewed child sexual abuse media, you have committed a crime against a child. You are a perpetrator of sexual abuse. These are the hard truths that you need to hear someone say out loud to you. We don't say these things to hurt you, or to shame you any further, but instead to help you accept the gravity of your online sexual offense behavior.

Part of the reason we are being so direct is that we often hear men say that the act of viewing child sexual abuse media is a "victimless" crime. Nothing could be further from the truth. One litmus test for assessing the true gravity of your behavior can be listening to yourself talk about your online sexual offense behavior. As you do, try to catch yourself using words such as "but...," or "however...," "even so...," "yet...," "in spite of that...," and other similar phrases. These qualifiers are all signs that you are minimizing the harm of your online sexual offense behavior.

The purpose of this chapter is to help you better understand that the viewing of child sexual abuse media has many real victims and is just as damaging as sexual abuse. In some cases, it can even feel more harmful to its victims than the act of sexual abuse itself. Later in this chapter, we will read a letter from one of the victims of child sexual abuse media to help you see how this can be true.

This chapter may be difficult for you to complete. It will challenge both the ways you think about the children victimized by child sexual abuse media, and the ways you think about yourself. Try to remember that growth comes from discomfort. If the chapter becomes too emotional for you, you can always take a break and talk to a trusted friend or professional. If we are striking a chord, it is probably one that needs to be struck!

A List of Chapter Exercises

1. Illusions: Perspective Matters
2. Please Leave a Message…
3. Half-Truths
4. Facing the Truth
5. Ripples
6. It's Time to Give Back

Don't Forget!

Those who have access to the Internet may want to visit our companion website for resources related to this and other chapters in the workbook. These resources include additional articles, websites, and copies of activities/graphics from the chapters.

http://www.internetbehavior.com/illegalimages

Notes

_____

_____

_____

_____

_____

_____

Illusions: Perspective Matters

Having fun with optical illusions… we've all done it. In the picture to the left, do you see a young lady or an old lady? It's both! It depends on the way you look at it… how your eyes process it… how your brain transforms the information.

Here's another optical illusion:

Can you see the face on the left? Just by rotating the face counterclockwise by 90 degrees, it suddenly becomes the word "Liar."

Okay, we admit it—we're quite fond of these illusions. But a major reason for that is they remind us that perspective-taking is a vital skill, especially when it comes to recognizing and accepting the experiences of others.

Let's start with a basic definition: Perspective-taking is the practice of intentionally adopting another person's point of view. It is the ability to understand and consider the thoughts, feelings, and experiences of others. Perspective-taking can help you better understand others' experiences and shift your own thoughts and feelings about a current situation or a person involved in that situation.

Are you the type of person that…

- Criticizes others without imagining being in their shoes?
- Doesn't listen to others because you KNOW you're right?
- Doesn't believe there are two sides to every story?
- Has your mind made up before the other person even begins to talk?
- Doesn't ever apologize?

If you are saying, "No, that's not me!" then wouldn't it make sense that you would have been more capable to see the harm you were causing others when you viewed child sexual abuse media? Maybe it is you. If you said, "Yes! That's me!" then we have some work to do. Either way, you need more information on perspective-taking.

Here are some basic steps to increase your skill at perspective-taking.

1. **Be willing to listen.** When in a dialogue with another person, you likely already have an opinion or perspective on the current situation. That opinion will not be able to change if you don't open yourself up to HEAR others. If you listen, you may learn something new, not just about the other person, but more importantly, about yourself.

2. **Ask more questions.** Be curious about the world around you and the people you are talking to. Asking questions not only helps you learn new things, but it can also expand your perspective and horizons in the world.

3. **Spend time with people.** Seeking out new people will offer you a different view of the world. Keep the people you meet diverse. Do Christians bother you? Spend time with them. Do you have difficulty understanding the LGBTQ community? Spend time with that gay friend you have. And when you meet with them… see #1 and #2 above.

4. **Read more and read broadly.** Books, magazines, and newspapers can all offer you a new and refreshing perspective. Even if you don't agree with the editorial, can you see their point of view? Reading = perspective building.

5. **Watch different stuff.** New TV shows, movies, try a different channel (food channel, home and garden, history, etc.) The world is an amazing place, but you won't be able to take different perspectives into account if you don't know the world.

6. **Use a new filter or new glasses to "see" the world.** Look for situations that you don't understand and try to understand them. Look for surprises. Think consistently and consciously about the new perspectives you've encountered and think about how you might be able to create new visions for yourself.

Reflect & Respond

1. Where did you learn your perspective-taking skills? What were your parents like? What did they teach you about perspective-taking? Did your perspective matter as a child? Did you witness the six perspective-taking skills mentioned above in your parents and other family members?

    _____

    _____

    _____

2. How would you rate your perspective-taking skills on a scale of 1 (really bad) to 10 (really good)? Justify your rating in the space below.

    It may be helpful to ask others who know you well. You may not have good perspective-taking skills when it comes to rating your perspective-taking skills. 🙂

    _____

    _____

    _____

3. How does this discussion of perspective-taking apply to child sexual abuse media? Are you able to take the perspective of the children in the images and videos you have seen? How would you rate your perspective-taking skills as they relate to your use of child sexual abuse media, on a scale of 1 (really bad) to 10 (really good)?

If you rated yourself a 1 on this last question, don't despair! There are lots of effective exercises in this chapter designed to help you develop the perspective needed to recognize the harm done to children who are victims of child sexual abuse and child sexual abuse media.

_____

_____

_____

React #1

For the next week, take time to observe as many discussions between people as possible. Observing discussions between people at work or at family gatherings can be a good place to start. Discussions between people on talk shows, TV shows, or in movies also provide good avenues for listening to people talk about their unique perspectives.

As you observe, note how others engage in, or maybe don't engage in, perspective-taking. What are signs that others are engaging in perspective-taking or not engaging in perspective-taking?

Jot down notes of your observations in the space below.

Notes

_____

_____

_____

_____

Look at the above list of six basic steps to increase your perspective-taking skills. Choose two things from the list and commit to purposefully engaging in those activities for the next week. Jot down notes of your experience in the space below.

Notes

_____

_____

_____

_____

_____

_____

_____

_____

_____

_____

_____

_____

Please Leave a Message...

The messages we receive in childhood often end up having an enormous impact on our ability to empathize with others. It is important to understand how the messages you received during your childhood impact your ability to understand and empathize with those you victimized with your use of child sexual abuse media.

Consider the following:

1. You grew up in a family where others did not express understanding or empathy for you. When bad things happened to you, your family members may have said things such as, "Just get up and dust yourself off," "Stop feeling sorry for yourself," "Be strong," "It is not that bad," or some version of these messages.

   This type of environment minimizes the feelings and struggles you experienced and likely makes it difficult as an adult for you to understand why the victimization of others is a "big deal." After all, shouldn't they just be able to "suck it up," like you had to do?

   If you grew up with these types of messages, you may experience:

   • Difficulties recognizing emotions
   • Struggles with being vulnerable
   • Excessive self-blame
   • Difficulties with intimacy
   • A lack of understanding and empathy for others

2. The second possibility is that you grew up in a family where other people never took any responsibility. Family members may have said, "Bad things always happen

to us," "People always take advantage of us," "It is not our fault," "We are not to blame," or some version of these messages.

This environment makes it difficult to step outside of yourself and take responsibility for the pain you may be causing others.

If you grew up with these messages, you may experience:

- Difficulties with taking responsibility and accountability
- Blaming others
- Making excuses for problems and challenges in your life
- Feeling like the world is out to get you
- Difficulties with intimacy

These roles make it difficult to understand how you may harm others. The first role doesn't allow you to recognize your victimization of others because you minimize the impact of victimization and have difficulties understanding how others are impacted. The second role assumes you bear no responsibility for the victimization. You stay focused on how you have been victimized rather than considering the impact of your victimization on others.

If you can identify with one of these roles, then you are on your way toward understanding the impact of your behavior on others. This self-awareness is the first step toward recognizing how your beliefs related to the victimization of others interfere with understanding the harm you have caused by your use of child sexual abuse media.

Reflect & Respond

1. Which of the two roles described above applies most to you? How does this role affect your life and your relationships with others? If neither role seems to fit, what other ways might your approach to the world have limited your ability to see the pain of others?

   _____

   _____

   _____

2. How do you think your childhood shaped your view of victimization—both your own and that of others? What messages did you receive about those who are victimized and those who cause harm? How have these messages impacted you?

   _____

   _____

   _____

3. How does your perception of victimization interfere with your ability to recognize the harm you have done to your partners, family, and friends through your use of child sexual abuse media?

   _____

   _____

   _____

4. How does your perception of victimization interfere with your ability to recognize the harm you have caused to the children who are victims of child sexual abuse media? If your answer is, "It doesn't," please start at the top and redo this exercise.

   _____

   _____

   _____

React

Now that you have examined and reflected on your own messages and attitudes related to victimization, take time to reflect on the harm you have caused—not only to the children in the images but also to your partner, family, and friends.

Remember, one role minimizes the feelings and struggles you have experienced, making it difficult for you to understand why the victimization of others is a "big deal." The other role makes it difficult to step outside of yourself, take responsibility, and recognize the pain you have caused others.

Make a list of ways you have harmed your partner, family and friends.

_____

_____

_____

_____

_____

_____

_____

_____

_____

_____

_____

Make a list of the ways you have harmed the children in the child sexual abuse media.

_____

_____

_____

_____

_____

_____

_____

_____

_____

_____

_____

_____

_____

Half-Truths

When we engage in behaviors that bring us pleasure, we often seek out ways to continue engaging in those same behaviors. If you like going out to eat, you will probably find opportunities to go out to eat more. If you enjoy gambling, then you may find it easy to come up with reasons to visit the casino. If you have made time to view child sexual abuse media, you most likely have used a half-truth to justify your behavior.

Look at some of these common half-truths:

> *I only look at AI-generated sexualized images of children, no harm in that.*
>
> *The stuff I look at is "art erotica." It's legal, so it's not problematic.*
>
> *Kids took these photos of themselves. Nobody abused or forced them.*
>
> *I only view images and videos of adolescents. It's normal.*
>
> *Viewing child sexual abuse media is not the same as touching a child.*
>
> *Hentai (cartoons) of sexualized children aren't real, so it's not a problem.*
>
> *Nobody is harmed by my viewing child sexual abuse media.*
>
> *The kids I watch are above the age of consent to have sex, so it's fine.*
>
> *I'm not really a sex offender since I didn't touch a child.*
>
> *Teens who post sexualized media of themselves are not being abused.*

These are called half-truths (not myths) because there may be a nugget of truth in the statement, but then we sprinkle on some "thought distortion" to try and make the whole statement true. If we can convince ourselves these are "truths," then we can continue to justify our behaviors.

For example, AI images, cartoons, and erotic art may not be illegal, but it is still unhealthy to continue to view, masturbate, and reinforce the sexualization of children. The sexualization of children is always unhealthy, no matter what form it takes.

One of the most common half-truths people use is "at least I didn't touch a child." While that may be true, the fact remains that someone did coerce and abuse the child. It's almost worse… it's like being a bystander and encouraging the abuse to occur.

Or what about selfies? You might say, "These kids recorded these images of themselves and posted them online. Obviously, they knew someone like me would look at the images and watch the videos. There is no victim, right?" Except what would make a child do that? The teen in the sexual media is likely experiencing some psychological distress or some type of abuse in their life, and you are choosing to exploit that distress or abuse by viewing the photos or watching the videos.

Are you guilty of half-truths to justify your viewing of child sexual abuse media? It's time to figure out the truth and start speaking and living it. Embracing the whole truth is the only way to gain awareness and empathy for the children victimized by child sexual abuse media.

Reflect & Respond

1. Do you use half-truths in other areas of your life? What is some behavior, other than viewing child sexual abuse media, that you justify by using "half-truths" in order to ignore the consequences to yourself and others? The more you practice disputing your half-truths in other areas of your life, the better you will become at disputing the half-truths you use when it comes to viewing child sexual abuse media.

_____

_____

_____

2. Think of a good friend or family member who uses half-truths in their life. What do they tell you or themselves about their bad habits? Something like, "I've been smoking my whole life; it's not going to do any good to quit now," or "Shopping is my only vice. I need something to feel better." Do you have other examples?

_____

_____

_____

If you can identify the half-truths others tell themselves, you will be better equipped to identify the half-truths you use. Write your observations of others' half-truths below.

Note You may not necessarily want to confront your friends or family members about their half-truths, especially at a gathering in front of everybody. 🙂

_____

_____

_____

3. How does learning to acknowledge the entire truth help you increase your awareness and empathy for the victims of child sexual abuse media?

_____

_____

_____

_____

_____

React

In the circle below, list half-truths in the light grey area that are related to your viewing of child sexual abuse media, and convert them into undisputed whole truths on the right (white) side of the circle. Choose half-truths that apply to you from the list we provided and create a couple of your own.

Show your circle to a trusted friend, therapist, or accountability partner and explain your process of converting the half-truths to the whole truth. Also, explain how you will continue to reinforce the whole truth with regard to your viewing child sexual abuse media and in your life in general.

Facing the Truth

 It's not easy to take the perspective of a child who has been victimized by child sexual abuse media. The images and videos make the kids seem distant and detached from your reality. In order to bridge this gap, researchers and legal professionals have gathered letters and statements from previously victimized children, so others can hear in their own words how their experience of child sexual abuse media has taken a major psychological toll on their lives.

The letter below is from a young woman who was sexually abused as a child. Photos of her abuse were then circulated and exchanged on the Internet over many years. This is a letter that is often used in court cases to help those in the justice system understand the long-term impact of child sexual abuse media.

I am a 19 year old female and I am a victim of child sex abuse and child pornography. I am still discovering all the ways that the abuse and exploitation I suffered has hurt me, has set my life on the wrong course, and destroyed the normal childhood, teenage years, and early adulthood that everyone deserves.

My uncle started to abuse me when I was only 4 years old. He used what I now know are the common ways that abusers get their victims ready for abuse and then silence them; he told me that I was special, that he loved me, and that we had our own "special secrets." Since he lived close to our house, my mother and father didn't suspect anything when I walked over there to spend time with him.

At first he showed me pornographic movies and then he started doing things to me. I remember that he put his finger in my vagina and that it hurt a lot. I remember that he tried to have sex with me and that it hurt even more. I remember telling him that it hurt. I remember that much of the time I was with him I did not have clothes on and that sometimes he made me dress up in lingerie. And I remember the pictures he would take of me.

After the abuse he would take me to buy my favorite snack, which was beef jerky. Even now when I eat beef jerky I get feelings of panic, guilt, and humiliation. It's like I can never get away from what happened to me.

At the time I was confused and knew it was wrong and that I didn't like it, but I also thought it was wrong for me to say anything bad about my uncle who said he loved me and bought me things I liked. He even let me ride on his motorcycle. I will never ride on a motorcycle again. The memories are too upsetting.

There is a lot I don't remember, but now I can't forget because the disgusting images of what he did to me are still out there on the Internet. For a long time I practiced putting the terrible memories away in my mind. Sometimes I just go into my mind. Thinking about it is still really painful. Sometimes I just go into staring spells when I am caught thinking about what happened and not paying any attention to my surroundings.

Every day of my life I live in constant fear that someone will see my pictures on the Internet and recognize me and that I will be humiliated all over again. It hurts me to know someone is looking at them - at me - when I was just a little girl being abused for the camera. I did not choose to be there, but now I am there forever in pictures that people are using to do sick things. I want it all erased. I want it all stopped. But I am powerless to stop it just like I was powerless to stop my uncle.

When they first discovered what my uncle did. I went to therapy and thought I was getting over this. I was very wrong. My full understanding of what happened to me has only gotten clearer as I have gotten older. My life and my feelings are worse now because the crime has never really stopped and will never really stop because of the online photos.

It is hard to describe what it feels like to know that at any moment, anywhere, someone is looking at pictures of me as a little girl being abused by my uncle and is getting some kind of sick enjoyment from it. It's like I am being abused over and over and over again.

I find myself unable to do the simple things that other teenagers handled easily. I do not have a driver's license. Every time I say I am going to do it, I don't. I can't plan well. My mind skips out on me when I think about moving forward with my life. I have been trying to get a job, but I just keep avoiding things. Forgetting it is the thing I do best since I was forced as a little girl to live a double life and was forced to "forget" what was happening to me. Before I realize it, I miss interviews or other things that will help me get a job.

Sometimes things remind me of the abuse and I don't even realize it until it is too late. For example, I failed anatomy in high school. I simply could not think about the body because of what happened to me. The same thing happened in college. I went to a psychology class where we watched a video about child abuse. Without even realizing why, I just stopped going to class. I failed my freshman year of college and moved back home.

It's easy for me to block out my feelings and avoid things that make me uncomfortable. I don't know when I will be ready to go back to college because I have huge problems with avoiding anything that makes me uncomfortable or reminds me of my abuse.

I am always scared that people will look at me and tell that I am a victim of sex abuse because my abuse is a public fact. I am worried that when my friends are on the Internet they are going to come across my pictures and it fills me with shame and embarrassment.

I am humiliated and ashamed that there are pictures of me doing horrible things with my uncle. Everywhere I go I feel judged. Am I the kind of person who does this? Is there something wrong with me? Is there something sickening and disgusting about who I am?

I am embarrassed to tell anyone what happened to me because I'm afraid they will judge me and blame me for it. I live in a small town and I think that if one person knows then everyone will know. I am just living in fear of the day someone sees those awful pictures of me and "the secret" about me will be out. It's like my life is on hold and I am frozen in time waiting. I know those disgusting pictures of me are stuck in time and are there forever for everyone to see.

I had terrible nightmares for a long long time. I would wake up sweating and crying and go to my parents for comfort. Now I still get flashbacks sometimes. There are thoughts in my head that are memories of the things that my uncle did to me. My heart will start racing and I will feel sweaty and then a stronger picture will pop up in my head and I have to leave the situation I am in. I have heard the voice of my uncle in my mind still talking to me saying, "don't tell, don't tell, don't tell." Thinking and knowing that the pictures of this are still out there just makes it worse. It's like I can't escape from the abuse, now or ever.

Because I've had so many bad dreams, I find it hard to sleep when it's dark. I like to keep the lights on thinking that will protect me from bad dreams. I hate scary movies and sometimes have nightmares for days.

Sometimes I have unreasonable fears that prevent me from doing the normal things that other kids do. My friends once asked me to go with her and her uncle to an amusement park. I could not get it out of my mind that I would be abused. In the end I just couldn't go. I kept wondering if my friend's uncle had seen my pictures? Did he know me? Did he know what I did? Is that why he invited me to the amusement park?

Trust is a very hard thing for me and often people just make me uncomfortable. I had to quit a job I had as a waitress because there was a guy who I thought was always staring at me. I couldn't stop thinking, did he recognize me? Did he see my pictures somewhere? I was simply too uncomfortable to keep working there.

Because of the way my uncle bribed me to perform sex acts on camera, I have trouble taking gifts from anyone. I always feel that people will expect something from me if they give me a present. This makes it difficult in my relationship with friends.

I want to have children someday, but it frightens me terribly to think about how I could keep them safe. Who could I possibly trust? Their teacher? Their coach? I don't know if I could ever trust anyone with my children. And what if my children and their friends see my pictures on the Internet? How could I ever explain to them what happened to me?

I am very confused about what love is, my uncle said he loved me and I wanted that love. But I know now that what he did to me is not love. But how will I be able to tell in the future if it is real love or just another person trying to exploit me and use me?

The truth is, I am being exploited and used every day and every night somewhere in the world by someone. How can I ever get over this when the crime that is happening to me will never end? How can I get over this when the shameful abuse I suffered is out there forever and being enjoyed by sick people?

I am horrified by the thought that other children will probably be abused because of my pictures. Will someone show my pictures to other kids, like my uncle did to me, then tell them what to do? Will they see me and think it's okay for them to do the same thing? Will some sick person see my picture and then get the idea to do the same thing to another little girl? These thoughts make me sad and scared. I blame myself a lot for what happened. I know I was so little, but why didn't I know better? Why didn't I stop my uncle? Maybe if I had stopped it there wouldn't be so many pictures out there that I can never take back or erase. I feel like I have to live with it forever and that it's all my fault.

I feel like I am unworthy of everything and a failure. What have I been good for except to be used by others over and over again. That's one of the reasons I haven't been able to get a job or stay in school. I'm tired of disappointing myself. I've already had enough disappointment for a lifetime and just don't want any more failure. To me this brings back all the terrible feelings and shame of abuse and exploitation.

Sometimes I deal with my feelings by trying to forget everything by drinking too much. I know this isn't good, but my humiliation and angry feelings are there with me all the time and sometimes I just need a way to make them go away for a while.

I feel like I have always had to live a double life. First I had to lie about what my uncle was doing to me. Then I had to act like it didn't happen because it was too embarrassing. Now I always know that there is another "little me" being seen on the Internet by other abusers. I don't want to be there, but I am. I wish I could go back in time and stop my uncle from taking those pictures, but I can't.

Even though I am scared that I will be abused or hurt again because I am making this victim impact statement, I want the court and judge to know about me and what I have suffered and what my life is like. What happened to me hasn't gone away. It will never go away. I am a real victim of child pornography and it affects me every day and everywhere I go.

Please think about me and think about my life when you sentence this person to prison. Why should this person, who is continuing my abuse, be free when I am not free?

Try to put yourself into the shoes of this young woman. Try to imagine her feelings and how child sexual abuse media has impacted, and continues to impact, her life today. Next, think about all the images and videos you have seen, all the child sexual abuse media, and try to imagine how your actions have impacted, and continue to impact, the lives of each of child in those images and videos. As was stressed by author of this letter - each time that image or video is viewed, she feels like she is being abused all over again.

Your insights into and feelings for victims of child sexual abuse images should be reflected in your responses to the Reflect & Respond questions and the React.

Reflect & Respond

1. What were your thoughts and feelings as you were reading the letter?

   _____

   _____

   _____

2. What was the most impactful part of the letter for you?

   _____

   _____

   _____

3. How do you feel this letter will impact your thoughts, feelings, and behaviors related to child sexual abuse media?

   _____

   _____

   _____

   _____

   _____

   _____

   _____

   _____

React

It is important that you spend significant time thinking about this exercise. This should not be a project that you just "phone in" or "throw together." It may be a good idea to talk to your therapist or other trusted people in your life before you start on this project.

We would like you to create some type of response to this letter. It can be a letter to the young woman who wrote this letter, or a letter to someone you've seen online and still think about. You may want to create a collage of some type. You may want to write a poem or a song. You may want to find music that reflects your feelings after reading the victim impact letter.

You can honor this letter in any way you choose. We only ask that you make it a response that is meaningful to you.

EXTRA CREDIT Read the article from the Crimes Against Children Research Center titled, "The Complex Experience of Child Pornography Survivors." The article can be found on the workbook's companion site, www.internetbehavior.com/illegalimages.

Notes

_____

_____

_____

_____

_____

_____

_____

Ripples

It is important to understand that your use of child sexual abuse media impacts not only the victims of these images and videos, but many others around you, including the community at large.

Imagine a calm lake, its surface smooth and undisturbed. When you throw a pebble into the lake, it creates small waves, or ripples, that spread outward in all directions from the point of impact. These ripples often reach much further than you might expect, and they also affect a progressively wider area as they move further and further away from where the pebble was first dropped.

In this analogy, the **pebble** represents your use of child sexual abuse media. The **ripples** symbolize the consequences of your use of child sexual abuse media, which spread out over time and affect more and more people, places, or situations.

The **lake** represents the world around you, in which your use of child sexual abuse media occurred. This lake can include many aspects of your environment, such as in your family or the larger community.

This is called "The Ripple Effect."

The Ripple Effect illustrates that small actions can have widespread impact. Even a tiny pebble creates ripples that reach far and wide, illustrating how seemingly minor actions can influence the broader system. Viewing even a small number of sexual abuse images or videos can have a large impact on you and others.

As the ripples expand, they touch areas further from the origin, demonstrating how consequences can spread beyond the immediate surroundings and impact people we may not even know.

This Ripple Effect occurs immediately whenever you use child sexual abuse media. The consequences begin with the victim of the child sexual abuse media, who experiences feelings of shame, guilt, anxiety, depression, and trauma. All feelings that can persist over time. They experience a disruption of their trust and their relationships. They develop negative coping mechanisms such as substance use or self-harming behaviors.

The Ripple Effect continues with YOUR family, who experience confusion, helplessness, shame, and anger. They experience additional stressors related to financial and logistical support. They experience abandonment and fear over the future.

The Ripple Effect grows larger with the impact on your friends and others who care about you. It grows even larger with the impact on your job, coworkers, and supervisors. It affects your faith community, and your hobbies and leisure life.

Finally, the Ripple Effect impacts your entire community by sowing fear, mistrust, and anger in your community members, as a result of them learning about your viewing of child sexual abuse media. It perpetuates the continued abuse of children and the view that online child sexual abuse media is available. The community spends time and money on your crime, pulling resources away from more productive endeavors.

React

Look at the image of the pond below. At the center of the ripple, write out the impact that using child sexual abuse media has on the children in the images and videos.

In the next circle out from the inner circle, list the impact that using child sexual abuse media has on your immediate family - your spouse or partner, your children, your parents, your siblings. Your loved ones.

In the next circle out, list the impact that using child sexual abuse media has on your close friends and the other people who care about you.

In the next circle out, list the impact that using child sexual abuse media has on your job, your co-workers, and the acquaintances in your life.

In the next circle out, list the impact that using child sexual abuse media has on your community.

When you are finished with this activity, you should have five separate ripples, each of which indicates the impact your use of child sexual abuse media has on the victim, your family, your friends, your job, your co-workers, your employer, your acquaintances, and your community.

Understanding this Ripple Effect, and how it follows directly as a result of your use of child sexual abuse media, is an important part of developing awareness of all the people and systems you have impacted with your choices and behavior.

Reflect & Respond

1. As you look at your pond, what are your thoughts and feelings about the Ripple Effect of your behavior?

_____

_____

_____

2. What are your biggest regrets as you look at the Ripple Effect of your use of child sexual abuse media?

_____

_____

_____

3. Do you have any ideas about what you can do to make amends to some of the people who have been impacted by your use of child sexual abuse media? This will be discussed further in another exercise, but it never hurts to start thinking about this now.

_____

_____

_____

Notes

_____

_____

_____

_____

_____

_____

_____

It's Time to Give Back

After seeing The Ripple Effect of your use of child sexual abuse media, you are probably beginning to understand that it is important to give back and make amends to your community and the people you have harmed.

Giving back and making amends requires a balance of accountability, empathy, and meaningful action, all of which demands respecting the boundaries and needs of both the victims of child sexual abuse media, as well as the larger community as a whole.

Before giving back, you need to be sure you have "done your work." If you continue to struggle with your use of child sexual abuse media, then you are not ready to tackle giving back and making amends.

Additionally, talk about this process with your therapist, accountability people, support group, faith leaders, and other trusted individuals. They can assist you in determining if you are ready to begin taking the appropriate steps.

Below are some ways you can give back and make amends for your use of child sexual abuse media. It is important to remember that whatever you choose, it should be a thoughtful and meaningful process for YOU.

Before you begin your "giving back" process, you need to make sure you are ready. There needs to be personal accountability in your recovery. Be sure you have committed to some form of professional help, that you have educated yourself about the impact of child sexual abuse media, and that you have accountability partners in your recovery.

Once you are ready to begin the give-back-and-make-amends process, consider the following ideas:

Community Service and Contribution

- **Volunteer Work (Non-Direct Roles):** Engage in community service projects that allow for contribution without direct interaction with vulnerable populations (e.g., environmental clean-up, food banks, or animal shelters).
- **Skill-Based Contributions:** Use professional or technical skills to assist non-profits or community initiatives.

Advocacy and Awareness

- **Promote Education:** Work with experts to create educational content related to the prevention of online child sexual abuse media.
- **Share Your Story (When Appropriate):** In cases where it is constructive and supported by professionals, sharing personal experiences of rehabilitation can serve as a deterrent and educate others.

Indirect Support for Victims

- **Financial Contributions:** Donate to organizations that offer counseling, shelter, or legal support to victims.
- **Support Prevention Programs:** Advocate for and support programs aimed at reducing sexual violence in the community.
- **Mentorship or Advocacy (With Caution):** After demonstrating a long history of rehabilitation and consulting with your therapist and your accountability group, you may choose to guide others through recovery and prevention paths.

Important Considerations

- **Boundaries and Restrictions:** Your process of giving back and making amends should not put victims or vulnerable populations at risk, or make victims feel unsafe.
- **Professional Guidance:** Any efforts should be guided by qualified professionals (e.g., therapists, legal advisors, or restorative justice facilitators) to ensure appropriateness and effectiveness.
- **Focus on Community and Systemic Change:** Encouraging systemic improvements, such as supporting education or advocating for legal reforms, can have a lasting impact without direct victim interaction.

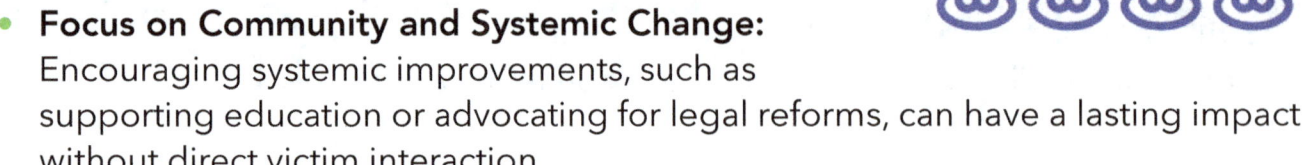

Finally, you must ENJOY! this process. After all, you have made it to a place in recovery where you can contribute back to the world. It's a long journey to get to this place, so find ways to give back and make amends that make you feel good! After all, you deserve it!!

Reflect & Respond

1. What are your initial thoughts about this idea of giving back and making amends meaningfully?

_____

_____

_____

_____

2. Do you feel like you are ready for this step, or do you need to do more work in understanding your sexually abusive behavior? What will move you toward being more ready?

_____

_____

_____

3. What ideas on the list above appeal to you? Do you have some other ideas?

_____

_____

_____

React

Creating a Personal Code of Conduct for Giving Back and Making Amends

Write a personal code of conduct that outlines how you will live moving forward. Include:

1. Specific behaviors you will avoid while engaging in the amends process. If you violate these behaviors, the give back should stop.

2. Steps you will take to ensure accountability (e.g., attending therapy, joining support groups) while you are engaged in the process of giving back and making amends.

Create an Action Plan

1. Research organizations in your area that allow volunteering without direct contact with vulnerable populations (e.g., food banks, environmental organizations).

2.   Create a plan to dedicate at least 5 hours a month to volunteering.

Include:

- The organization's name
- The type of service you will provide
- A schedule for your commitment

3.   Develop a proposal for supporting one of these programs (e.g., raising awareness, donating, fundraising, or volunteering).

_____

_____

_____

_____

_____

_____

_____

_____

_____

_____

_____

Conclusion: Reaching the Finish Line

Hooray! You made it!!! You finished the workbook… well, almost. There are a few final gifts to give yourself before you close the workbook (which we hope you will open again in the future, to review all your hard work). In fact, the following exercise is a way to summarize some of the main takeaways from the workbook. Keep in mind that these takeaways might change when you look back at the workbook again in the three months, six months, or a year.

Don't get too excited. This exercise is a little complicated and can be confusing…but we have faith in you! Believe us when we say the exercise will be worth it if you can stick with it. The reason we like this one so much is that it pulls everything together from the workbook AND gives you a plan for the future. Don't curse us…just do it!

To review, there are the six main concepts discussed in our workbook:

(1) Emotion Management

(2) Intimacy Skills

(3) Deviant Sexuality

(4) Out of Control Sexual Behavior

(5) Technology Use

(6) Victim Awareness

Take a look at the *Illegal Images Workbook Overview* sheet below. You will notice there are six tables, one for each of the above areas. Please take the next few days or so to review each of the chapters of the workbook. On the worksheet below, write three challenges you faced in each area, as well as three solutions that will help you address those challenges.

Illegal Images Workbook Overview

Emotion Management			Out of Control Sexual Behavior	
Challenges	Solutions		Challenges	Solutions

Intimacy Skills			Technology Use	
Challenges	Solutions		Challenges	Solutions

Deviant Sexuality			Victim Awareness	
Challenges	Solutions		Challenges	Solutions

We have also placed a larger version of this worksheet at the end of this activity. You can use this larger, blank overview sheet to help you with this activity.

Once you have completed the overview sheet, there is a second exercise that will help you monitor your challenges and solutions. Remember when we said this exercise was a little complicated…here is your reminder that it is a little complicated, but hang in there! You'll be glad you did!

Below is a sample "Weekly Challenges/Weekly Solutions" sheet. We will pretend it belongs to "John." At the start of the week, John chose three challenges from his overview sheet and wrote them in the boxes at the bottom of the "Challenges" section. Then, he chose three solutions from his overview sheet and wrote them in the boxes on the bottom of the "Solutions" section.

He then placed an X on the vertical black lines above each box, representing how he was doing with those challenges and solutions at the start of his week. The higher John put the X, the more trouble he was having with that particular challenge or solution. Then, throughout the week, he reminded himself to focus on using his solutions to address his challenges.

On the left (challenges) side of the chart the line goes up from green to red, since the more difficult each challenge is, the higher the mark goes on the line. The line on the right (solutions) side of the chart goes up from red to green (opposite of the left line), since you want to "turn up" your solutions and mark them higher on the line while hoping your challenges decrease.

At the end of the week, he re-rated his challenges and solutions by placing a circle on the vertical line, to represent an average rating of how he did with his challenges and solutions throughout the week.

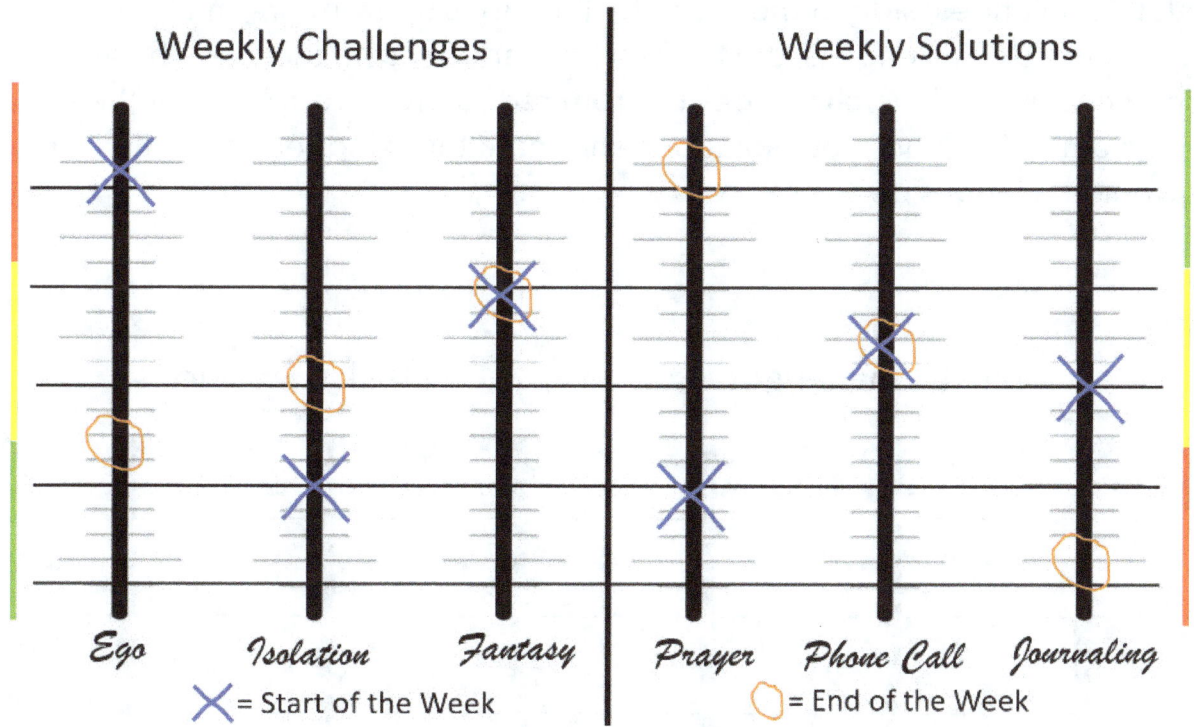

Finally, John took a step back and analyzed his chart, making a journal entry about things he noticed during his analysis. For example, at the start of the week John recognized that he was struggling with his ego, doing ok with his isolation, and having only minor issues with his fantasies. He also noted that he wasn't using his solutions very effectively at the start of the week. By the end of the week, he reported that he'd used prayer a great deal more during the week, made his normal amount of phone calls, and decreased his journaling. As a result, his problems with his ego decreased dramatically, while his isolation increased (probably a result of not connecting more with others), and his fantasy problems remained steady.

John can now use this information to create a new "Weekly Challenges/Weekly Solutions" sheet for his upcoming week. He can change his challenges and solutions or choose to leave them the same.

Now it is your turn. Use the "Weekly Challenges/Weekly Solutions" sheet to keep a steady eye on your recovery, focusing on the challenges you're facing and the solutions that work effectively to resolve those challenges. There is a blank copy of this sheet at the end of this conclusion for you to copy and use as much as you'd like.

NOTICE

On the left (challenges) side of the chart the line goes up from green to red, since the more difficult each challenge is, the higher the mark goes on the line. The line on the right (solutions) side of the chart goes up from red to green (opposite of the left line), since you want to "turn up" your solutions and mark them higher on the line while hoping your challenges decrease.

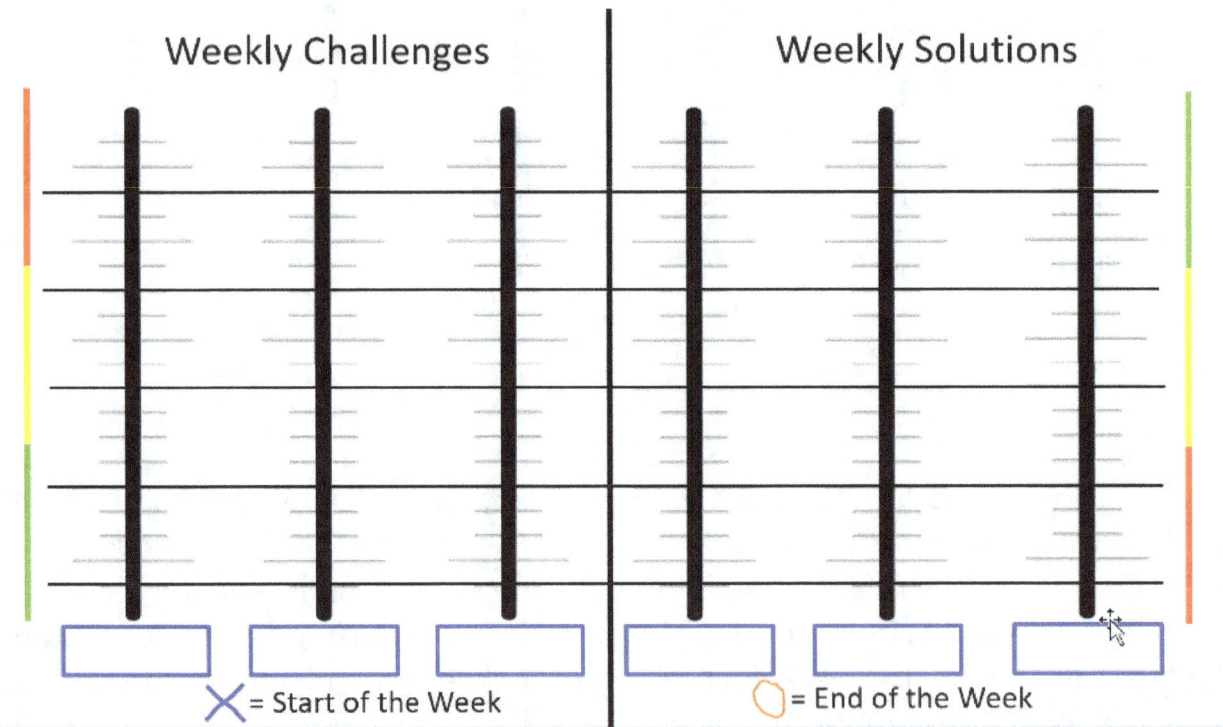

Illegal Images Workbook Overview

Emotion Management

Challenges	Solutions

Intimacy Skills

Challenges	Solutions

Deviant Sexuality

Challenges	Solutions

Out of Control Sexual Behavior

Challenges	Solutions

Technology Use

Challenges	Solutions

Victim Awareness

Challenges	Solutions

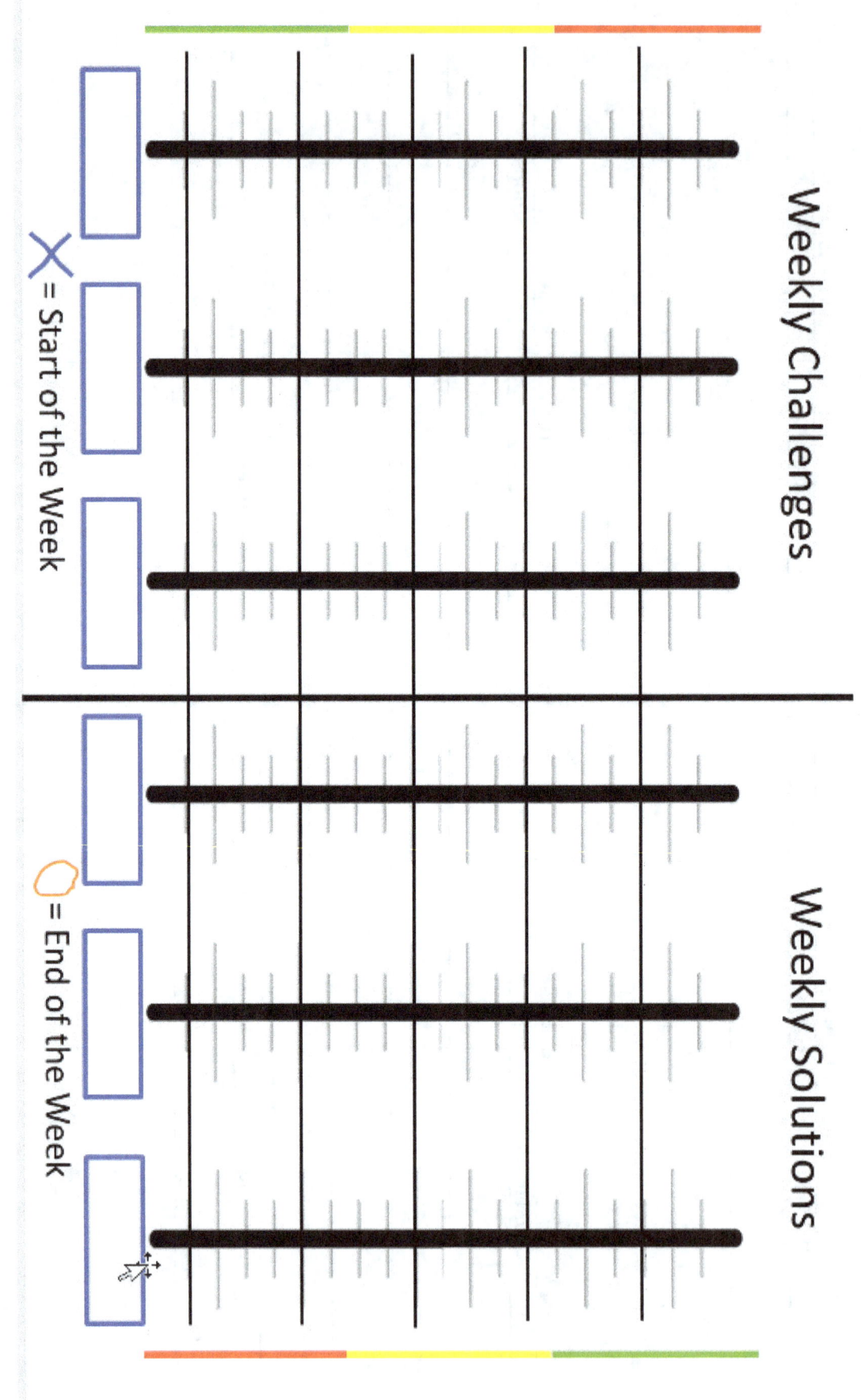

Weekly Challenges

Weekly Solutions

X = Start of the Week

◯ = End of the Week

Notes

A Final Note

This has been quite a journey. We are honored to have taken it with you. Thank you for trusting us to guide you. It is our desire that this workbook has led you on a path where you discovered some level of awareness, health, freedom, and hope - as represented on the cover of the book. See how we brought you full circle!

Don't Forget!

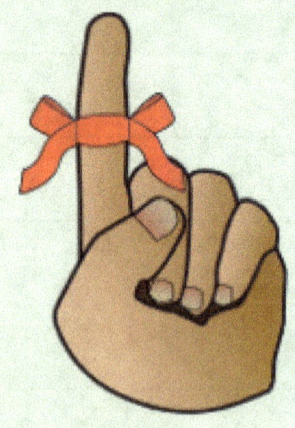

Those who have access to the Internet may want to visit our companion website for resources related to this and other chapters in the workbook. These resources include additional articles, websites, and copies of activities/graphics from the chapters.

http://www.internetbehavior.com/illegalimages

www.ingramcontent.com/pod-product-compliance
Lightning Source LLC
Chambersburg PA
CBHW081530120626
46550CB00009B/2671